How To Change Your Life

BOOKS BY ERNEST HOLMES

Can We Talk to God?

Change Your Thinking, Change Your Life

Creative Ideas

Creative Mind and Success

Effective Prayer

Good for You

How to Use the Science of Mind

Ideas for Living

It Can Happen to You

Questions and Answers on the Science of Mind

The Beverly Hills Lectures

The Magic of the Mind

The Science of Mind

The Science of Mind Approach to Successful Living

The Voice Celestial

This Thing Called Life

This Thing Called You

Thoughts Are Things

What Religious Science Teaches

Words That Heal Today

HOW TO CHANGE YOUR LIFE

Ernest Holmes

A Science of Mind Book

Health Communications, Inc.
Deerfield Beach, Florida

www.bcibooks.com

**Library of Congress Cataloging-in-Publication Data
is available through the Library of Congress.**

ISBN-13: 978-1-55874-686-2
ISBN-10: 1-55874-686-2

Publisher: Health Communications, Inc.
          3201 S.W. 15th Street
          Deerfield Beach, FL 33442-8190

R-03-07

Cover design by Larissa Hise

CONTENTS

II

*A deeper look at the life-changing power you have.
Some key Science of Mind perspectives.*

III

*Ideas about life and God essential to modern spiritual
understanding. Supportive quotations from the world's
timeless writings.*

IV

*How science and spirituality, once believed
to be antagonists, are coming together.*

V

*Step-by-step instructions on how to use the Science of Mind
for your personal need.*

VI

*Forty inspirational guides to solving problems and changing
your life. Followed by affirmations for specific application.*

PUBLISHER'S INTRODUCTION

This remarkable book contains some of the most powerful ideas you will ever read. If you sincerely apply them, you can have happiness, health, financial security, loving relationships and any other good things you desire. You can dissolve fear, stress and anxiety. And you can gain a greater insight into your true nature as a human being.

The author, Dr. Ernest Holmes (1887–1960), was one of America's outstanding spiritual teachers. Through lectures, radio and television programs, tape recordings, books and magazines, he introduced millions of people to the simple principles for successful living which he called "the Science of Mind."

Those principles, along with a technique for applying them, are thoroughly described in this book. Also included are many specific examples, so you can use the Science of Mind directly for your personal needs.

Are you ready to change your life for the better? If you are, you can start right now. You have found what you're looking for. Welcome to the Science of Mind!

FOREWORD

In *How to Change Your Life*, Dr. Ernest Holmes has given the world another spiritual classic. If you seem to experience lack, limitation, fear, worry or insecurity, take heart! Turn to any page within this book and you will realize that your experience is simply an idea shortage! There is nothing outside of yourself that is missing, if you will but look within to the vast storehouse of consciousness right at the center of your own being.

Embodying and practicing the universal truths in *How to Change Your Life* will teach you to tap directly into the spiritual laws that create, support and maintain the entire cosmos. Although this book was written in 1957, just as two and two will eternally equal four, so does truth, written during any age and time, equal truth.

Dr. Holmes was a great spiritual scientist who provides empirical evidence for his realizations of the original purpose of life. You, too, by experimenting in the laboratory of your own life using the techniques described in these pages, will prove as he did that thoughts are the things that create your life.

Dr. Ernest Holmes was a man of great spiritual passion and understanding. As you will experience, he taught universal principles in a way that offered them to people on all levels of the sacred journey, in all the stages of awakening.

So journey into a remarkable invisible realm that awakens your highest potential.

Reverend Dr. Michael Beckwith

I

Basic Ideas of
the Science of Mind

A simple explanation of why your thoughts have power. How you can change your life by changing your thinking.

Your Dreams Can Come True!

Every human being thrills at the thought of having dreams come true! The idea means different things to different people. To you it may mean physical health: the ability to walk, run, play, to engage in activity. To me, it may mean abundance: money, a home, a car—opulence. To another, dreams may involve education, or the ability to get along with people. Whatever your personal desires may be—as long as they do not hurt yourself or someone else—you have a right to attain them . . . *and you can.*

The ability to attain your goals—to control your experiences and have them result in happiness, prosperity and success—lies in your own mind and the way you use it. This means *you control your own experience*—you are really in charge of your affairs and the way they are to develop.

Let us sum it up this way: *My thought is in control of my experience, and I can direct my thinking.*

Read that again and then say it aloud. It is a most astounding statement and at first may even seem far-fetched. But because you are a thoughtful person with an open mind, ready to be shown what you may not at first understand—even what does not seem entirely believable—you will be willing to take that statement under consideration and hear the reasons for it. Certainly you do not have to believe it nor do you wish to until you have investigated it, heard the arguments in its favor, and observed whether or not it works for you after you have given it a fair trial. That is the way the intelligent mind approaches any new idea.

IT HAS TO MAKE SENSE

No one can force a new belief upon another; no one has the right to attempt to do so. Only when we have made the appropriate intellectual inquiries and investigations for ourselves can we honestly decide whether to accept or reject what is presented to us. We are not going to allow ourselves to be coerced into anything of which our own good judgment does not approve. However, we cannot bring our good judgment to bear upon anything in fullest measure until we have been fair in our efforts to understand it and then faithful in our attempts to test it, to see *if it actually does work for us.*

If you were raised under Christian influences in the home and church, you will probably feel particularly sensitive about things that sound religious. You will be inclined to say, "I do not want anything to disturb my faith in God as an Overruling Providence and in Jesus as the Wayshower for men and women through his practical application of a loving, useful life and his triumphant conquest even over death itself."

In response, the Science of Mind viewpoint suggests, "You are exactly right!"

On the other hand, if you have lived apart from church activities and associations, or you have found them unfitted to your intellectual turn of mind and you want something on which you can base your thinking and faith, something that retains a clear concept of the orderly world of science in which natural law and order prevail, then we say, "That is a rational viewpoint and we believe you will find much that is of interest and value to you in the Science of Mind."

Possibly, though, you may be just a busy man or woman who desires a wholesome, successful life and a sense of security. If you are going to give your attention to a new way of thinking, it will have to be something that makes sense and that you can apply in your everyday affairs, because you know it works!

This is a realistic and reasonable attitude according to the Science of Mind viewpoint.

SOMETHING FOR YOU

So . . . if an understanding of God meets your daily needs in a world of practical affairs, you want it. If some system of reasoning conforms to your keenest intellectual understanding and scientific knowledge, it is of interest to you. If you can find something which, for you, satisfies the deep inner hunger that lies in the hearts of all people (whether they ever acknowledge that hunger or not), you are just as eager as anyone else to find satisfaction. You have practical daily needs that must be met, intellectual demands that seek rational fulfillment, and sincere spiritual longings that have to be fulfilled. This is true of all persons. You are no exception.

Now that we have a foundation for mutual understanding

and a willingness to look into an exciting new way of thinking, let us go back to our earlier statement, enlarge it, and give it more careful consideration:

> *The ability to control my experiences and have them result in happiness, health, prosperity and success lies in my own mind and my use of it.*

HOW CAN THIS BE SO?

Physical science has proved that everything can be scientifically reduced to one ultimate invisible Essence, something which cannot be directly contacted by the physical senses. It is therefore only reasonable to say that originally everything must have come from that Essence. According to your own way of thinking, different names are given to It: Energy, Principle, Universal Intelligence, Universal Mind, Consciousness, Spirit, God.

For our purpose it does not particularly matter which of these names we use. Let us call It *Mind.* This probably has the broadest meaning for most of us, without too many limiting ideas connected with it.

Scientists show us that Energy—an aspect of Mind—is interchangeable with Substance, and is everywhere: within us, around us, filling all space to the limitless reaches of the universe.

Everything we can see, touch, taste, smell or contact in any physical way, we are told, is but some aspect of this Universal Energy or Mind, which has been channeled into specific and tangible form so that our senses become aware of It.

For instance, on a summer day, entirely invisible vapor arises from the ocean and soars high in the sky. By contacting a different air temperature it becomes a cloud. If colder air still further condenses it, it turns into raindrops which help fill a lake. In winter a further change takes place and instead of raindrops there are snowflakes. Winter also changes the water of the lake to ice. In every instance we have *only that original vapor*, though it has taken forms of which our senses are aware. Similarly, Universal Mind, though always basically the same, appears in many different forms.

MIND IS EVERYWHERE

Einstein's famous equation, $E=mc^2$, revolutionized and clarified much scientific thinking and at the same time cleared the way for the establishment of firmer foundations in philosophic and religious thought. In essence it means that energy and mass are one and the same, and are interchangeable. From our point of view this means that Mind–God–acting as Energy, becomes what we know as the physical world, according to law. *They are one and the same thing* (although God, being infinite, could never be depleted by what is created). We may reasonably declare that everything which will ever exist must also come from God. In fact there is nothing else out of which anything could be made.

Mind is everywhere! After all, this is just the same as what we were taught to say in earliest childhood: "God is everywhere." That statement may not have meant much to us then, but now we know that this Universal Mind is everywhere . . . *therefore It is within us!*

There can be no exception to that *everywhereness*. This gives us a key to the whole nature of Life and allows us to understand that not only our individual minds, but our bodies as well, are expressions and a part of Mind.

HOW YOU CAN UTILIZE
THIS NEW AWARENESS

At the beginning of this world system of ours, there must have been nothing but the great Universal Mind—God—and out of Itself the tangible universe was formed.

Those of us with Christian backgrounds were taught that God—Universal Mind—is omnipresent, and that we too were made in His image and likeness. So now we arrive at the conclusion that *we, at our level, possess a creativity similar to that of the Universal Mind.* We create in our experience whatever we choose: health, happiness, prosperity, employment—any good thing we need—through the process of our constructive thought, through which the unlimited creativity of Mind acts, giving form to our desired objective. The only way for us to constructively use the creativity of this invisible but everywhere-present Mind is *by means of our thought, faith and conviction*—and nothing else!

YOU HAVE A RIGHT TO CREATE

Today, the old idea of our being like God, the image-and-likeness concept, applies in a new and different but very important way. Since we are created of that which God is—Mind—we are made of and possess Godlike qualities, and we have the right and the ability to develop and use them. In fact, it is *necessary* for us to do this if we are to fully express the Life within us. Later we shall discuss these qualities, but just now we are interested in the creative aspect of our minds.

What you *choose* is created for you out of and through the action of the One Universal Mind, which is everywhere and is accessible to you. You avail yourself of the Creative Action of Mind through *what you believe!* Perhaps you are not quite ready to accept this statement, but it is an interesting one, and well worth remembering.

HOW CAN YOU LEARN TO BELIEVE?

First of all, you must remember that you can think whatever you please. No one can direct your thought processes. They are under your control.

Someone may say, "You must think as a Republican," or "You have to be a Democrat in your thinking," or "My church's way of thinking is the only right one; you must think that way also," or "When you see a blackboard you have to think of it as being white." All of this is ridiculous. You may have to make your *actions* conform to what those in authority tell you, but they simply cannot control your *thinking.* You will go on thinking just as you want to. In that respect you are independent, no matter where you live or what your circumstances may be.

If your thinking processes are really under your personal control, as you will agree they must be, and if thought is acted upon by the creativity of Mind to produce results according to your belief, then you surely do have the power to become the master of your own affairs and to bring to pass those good conditions you desire.

This makes the *omnipresence of God* and the *made in the image and likeness of God* very practical and important ideas rather than abstract theological concepts. They can now become important truths which are part of your everyday life and are therefore of prime importance in all the practical aspects of living.

Let us keep in mind that we not only have the God-given ability to do this kind of results-oriented thinking, but that we also have the *right* to do it. In connection with the God

Power within you, there are many other aspects, but this one—*the right and the ability and the power to "think creatively" so that you have more desirable experiences*—is so impressive and so exceedingly important that it should be the basis of your life. Even though you may not fully accept or understand this statement yet, you can begin to put it into actual application for yourself. You can start right now to make it work!

HE CHANGED HIS LIFE!

The true story is told of a man in one of our Eastern cities who had been in one job for twenty-five years at a very mediocre salary. He had become extremely dissatisfied, wanted to get out of the rut, but didn't know how to do it. When he accepted a few simple but profound ideas like these, he began to realize that he had the right and the ability to declare better conditions for himself. In less than one month from the time he began to think in this way—and to act accordingly—his salary was increased to exactly three times what it had been before!

When we get only a glimpse of the true nature of Mind—the God-Power within us—and use It, the results are truly amazing. Physically, financially, socially, intellectually and spiritually, it pays us to learn about and to use the principles of creative thinking. The student in a laboratory who tries a valid experiment and fails does not give up; he tries again and again until he proves it for himself. Shouldn't we be equally faithful in testing these scientific laws of Mind? Our personal welfare demands continued, faithful endeavor and experimentation.

There is but One Mind; It is Omnipresent—It is all there is. Everything visible and invisible is but a manifestation of this One Mind—the result of Its Creative Action and the becoming of that which It creates. Because *you* are made in the image and likeness of God, you can use your mind, according to its nature, and by choice bring your good to you.

A PICTURE OF YOUR MIND

Now examine the diagram below and think of it as representing the entire universe—all that is. All of it is Mind.

For the sake of clarity we divide it into three sections, but it is all Mind!

Part I, we may call Conscious Mind. Conscious Mind is that faculty with which you think and plan; with it you become aware of ideas, analyze, make decisions and carry on all mental processes. Let us think of it as being like the superintendent of a manufacturing plant, who thinks out what is to be done and gives instructions.

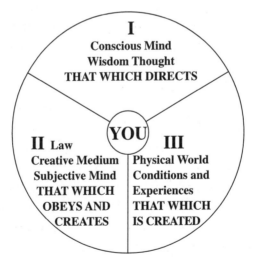

Needless to say, however, nothing could be accomplished if some department did not take those instructions and carry them out. So, Part II is the aspect of Mind that obeys the directions of Part I. Think of it as the manufacturing plant itself, where the instructions are taken and worked out. From the Science of Mind viewpoint, we call this the Subjective Mind, the Law which acts and creates automatically according to instructions. It obeys the directions of Part I. Without Part I, it would be useless because it would lack instructions. Without Part II, Part I would be helpless for want of something to take directions and bring them to fulfillment. One part, therefore, is just as important as the other.

Now look at Part III and realize that it is the only part of the universe you can experience—see, touch or contact with your physical senses. It is the realm of tangible things and conditions. Here are the *results* of what was directed by Part I and carried out by Part II. Parts I and II instigate and carry out; Part III is the result, or effect.

In the diagram, see the tiny portion marked "You." Notice that you, too, possess the three aspects of Mind: direction, creation, result.

Remember:

1. Everything is Mind and you are therefore a part of it.

2. Mind responds and produces according to *your* believing thought.

3. You have the right and power to think what you want to think; so, you may create good conditions for yourself and others.

4. *Therefore, you control your own good and may transform your life into an experience of happiness, health and prosperity.*

QUESTIONS FOR SELF-STUDY AND GREATER FOCUS

(Each chapter in Part I of this book is followed by questions. These questions are designed to help you apply Science of Mind principles to your life in a direct and personal way. Space has been provided for you to write your answers directly in the book, to assist you in deeper study and future reference.)

1. What does the average person want to get from studying about Universal Mind?

2. What is my particular desire as I read this book?

3. Why is the idea of the Omnipresence of God important to me?

4. How has modern science helped us understand the way we can control conditions?

5. What in this chapter has been of the greatest importance to me?

6. Can I see clearly any one thing I possess or condition in my life that is the direct result of my thinking?

2

Your Mind . . .
Your Health

The first thing you should do at this point is realize that you can achieve vibrant health through right thinking. At the very beginning—right now—a state of expectancy is a great asset; a state of uncertainty—one moment thinking "perhaps" and the next moment thinking "I don't know"—will never get desired results. Even God can give you nothing until you make up your mind about what you expect.

The principle involved in this approach to well-being may be summed up in the words: *Mind responds to mind.* It is done unto you as you believe. Therefore your bodily conditions are governed by your thought processes (an idea now widely corroborated by psychosomatic medicine).

In order to understand this principle so you can apply it, refer to the diagram at the end of the last chapter. We called

Part I the Conscious Mind, that aspect of Mind in us with which we do our thinking and reasoning.

We referred to Part II as the Subjective Mind. Subjective means "under the direction of" and this is true about that portion of Mind which acts as Law—It is the creative, obedient, formative Power (though this does not mean It is any less important). We need always remember that there is but One Universal Mind. Each one of us uses a portion of It. Really, each one of us *is* a portion of It, for all—everything— is Mind. Our designating Its different activities simply enables us to understand more easily the way It works and allows us to use It more intelligently.

OUR BODIES WORK AUTOMATICALLY

In considering the creation of health by right thinking, we first need to realize that, through Universal Law, the body is built and automatically maintained. Law is constantly at work sustaining God's perfect idea of health. It keeps us breathing, keeps our hearts beating, takes care of our temperature, circulates our blood, digests our food, eliminates refuse and does everything which keeps the marvelously intricate machinery of the body in operation. Universal Law is far wiser than any chemist in the world and is forever at work. It never sleeps, and in *our* sleep the Law takes care of all our physical needs and gets us into good condition for the activities of the waking hours to come. Certainly we owe a vast debt of gratitude to that obedient Law of Mind in Action. In thousands of ways It is eminently wise, for It does many things we could not possibly know enough about to direct It to do.

THE VALUE OF HABIT

There is a second way, however, in which Law works—and that is by acting on our habits. A habit is the result of something we have done with deliberate attention and conscious effort so many times that we do not now need to think specifically about it when doing it. That is, the Law of Mind responds to a persistent idea and automatically maintains it. We can talk and walk and do scores of different kinds of work and play while still thinking about other things. But we could not do so at first; we had to form persistent thought-patterns before these activities could be released from our conscious attention. In the matter of habits, we have found that this very accommodating and capable function of Mind will accept any thought pattern we persistently give to It and will, from then on, automatically maintain that pattern for us.

We are reasonable and wise to give over into Its care those things which would be advantageous to us. There are many attitudes and activities in which we ought to be more proficient, which would make us more agreeable companions, more capable workers, happier individuals—more skillful, adaptable and efficient. So we can be more healthy and more prosperous and we can advance our own well-being in many ways *by simply deciding what we desire to be or to do* and then giving the matter enough conscious attention so that it becomes a habitual thought-pattern. Then, the Law of Mind will maintain it for us, since the Law of Mind obeys conscious direction.

WATCH YOUR MENTAL ATMOSPHERE

Here is a phrase which describes one of the great, important and valuable ways in which our thought works: *Mind responds to mind.* Mind is Intelligence, and of course Intelligence responds to intelligence. We can put this principle into operation in regard to our health, either to prevent illness or to heal it after it has developed.

We all know that in the process of living, millions of body cells are replaced daily. Millions of new cells are constantly growing within our bodies, and they immediately take on the "atmosphere" of the surroundings in which they find themselves. The atmosphere or tone of the body may be either wholesome, happy, optimistic and, therefore, healthy— or the opposite: gloomy, apprehensive, frightened, fearful, anxious, discouraged, weak and sickly. This *atmosphere* is the sum total of the way we allow ourselves to think and feel. Maybe we are really ill. If so, it is especially necessary that we give today's new cells the right, wholesome, happy atmosphere in which to live and work, for by doing so we get at least that much of our system into good order. If we can maintain a positive mental atmosphere, tomorrow's new cells added to today's supply will bring us that much nearer recovery.

Scientists assert that in only eleven months *all the cells* of the body are made new. So, day after day in thought, we can add to our experience of wholesomeness and health, and in this way redeem the whole body from illness. There is ample medical proof regarding the effect of sad, gloomy, anxious thoughts upon the general welfare and the functions of the body . . . and also proof about the healing power of right thinking. This is nothing we need to take on blind faith; it is scientifically verifiable knowledge.

The beliefs we have accepted—to which Law automatically responds—are continually being brought forth into our experience. The results are good health or illness, depending upon what we have believed. Because of this principle and our understanding of it, we can keep ourselves well, happy and free of disease; or if we have become ill, we can bring about the necessary healing. If the Science of Mind did nothing else for us, this alone would be an unspeakably great blessing.

EXPANDING OUR PERSPECTIVE

So far, we have been considering this from a very narrow viewpoint, as though we were keeping ourselves in that small circle in the diagram on page 11. But we need to remember that the small circle actually does not exist, that there is no barrier between ourselves and the Universal Mind, God. Let us remember that we are definite, distinct and particular expressions of God, individualizations of God, and have access to the whole of God-Wisdom and Power!

In order for us to bring to pass any specific result, there has to be a particular pattern of thought through which the result may manifest! *That pattern of thought is created by the way you think!* Your thinking is the creator of your experience! The unlimited, Universal Mind in you, as you, thinks and speaks and creates your good *through* you—when you are wise enough to permit It to.

Now you can declare your own health because you know you are of the Infinite. You may be assured of perfect results because what is termed "your mind" is an individualization of the One Mind and possesses Its creativity. That All-wise and All-powerful Mind flows creatively through you and can, by means of your belief and thought, fulfill your needs and supply a greater experience of good.

EXAMPLES OF RIGHT THINKING

Anyone who observes carefully will soon accumulate much evidence to prove that bodily illness is produced by wrong thinking and that it can be healed by *right* thinking.

The British Medical Journal has said: "There is not a tissue in the human body wholly removed from the influence of the spirit."

The former Chief Surgeon and Superintendent of the Clifton Springs Sanitorium at Clifton Springs, New York, said: "A large majority of the surgical cases that come to me should never really have come. They could have been headed off. . . . Wrong moral and mental attitudes created functional disturbances in the physical organism and these in turn became organic or structural disease. At this point I get them as a surgeon, but they could have been headed off. . . ."

E. A. Strecker, in his book *Mental Hygiene*, said: "Fully 50 percent of the problems of the acute stages of illness and 75 percent of the difficulties of convalescence have their primary origin not in the body, but in the mind of the patient."

Dr. Franz Alexander has said: "Hostility, suppressed for years, like a boiling volcano which never erupts, is the fundamental cause of malignant high blood pressure for which no physical cause has ever been found."

One doctor tells of a woman who greatly disliked her son-in-law, yet for the sake of seeing her daughter she visited in their home once each year. Every time she went she suffered from arthritis; after coming away from his presence, she recovered.

Hundreds of such examples could be given, but they do us very little good if we do not *prove the principle for ourselves.* The Law of Mind in action manifests for us the beliefs we speak into It. When we understand that there is a definite

Law with which we are working, it is much easier to have the faith required to bring healing. Remember, we are spiritual beings. The real "I," our special individuality, is God in us, as us . . . and as such must of course be perfect. This "I" functions through the intellect, the emotions and the body—all parts of one indivisible Whole.

IDEAS FOR YOU TO USE NOW

The following simple procedures, practiced daily in a persistent, happy and expectant manner, will soon produce a good effect upon your health:

Night and morning try to set apart a time in which to be quiet, to commune with your *real* self. This becomes the period in which you clarify your mental atmosphere. Be as relaxed physically as you can, but neither the position you occupy, the chair in which you sit, nor the room has anything to do with the real work you are doing. Merely see to it that there is no physical discomfort while you attempt to direct your thinking.

Now that some of the bodily tension, which is the bane of our anxious way of living, has been released, say with conviction and feeling:

I am strong and free through the Action of God in me.

I am well and successful in everything I do.

Repeat this until you feel the thrill of it all through you. It is a wonderful tonic.

After that, spend ten minutes thinking over some part of what you have read in this chapter, assimilating it more thoroughly . . . or have a quiet prayer time in which you do not *ask* for things or conditions, but name them, *accept* them as already belonging to you, and give *thanks* for them.

This whole procedure will probably take about twenty minutes. But will it be worthwhile? You would not start on a day's trip in your car without an adequate supply of gas and oil, would you? Why start out on your day's work without getting yourself properly supplied, physically, emotionally and spiritually?

A feeling of complete well-being will diffuse through you at the conclusion of this quiet time. See if you cannot keep this high consciousness all day.

BE PERSISTENT

Even if this process does not seem to mean much the first day or so, keep at it. It involves changing your whole way of life and it requires reeducating your body, your emotions, your intellect and your spiritual outlook. Be fair to yourself. Keep on doing it!

Plant deeply in your mind these four basic ideas:

1. You are completely surrounded by and are part of Universal Mind. Mind penetrates your very being; It is what you are.

2. This Mind is always creative, manifesting what you think and believe, as form or as some experience.

3. Universal Mind answers to your mind. Mind creates for you according to the pattern you make for It—by your thoughts of good or not-so-good. Your task, therefore, is to maintain only positive, uplifting, harmonious thoughts.

4. Because of this, you can choose to remain in good health, or to be healed if you are now ill. In the same

manner, you may choose and bring into your experience any other good condition.

To declare yourself into good health is one of the greatest blessings you could ever enjoy. The simple explanations given here are intended to start you on the way to such declarations, because you can now begin to understand what is needed to bring about healing.

QUESTIONS FOR SELF-STUDY AND GREATER FOCUS

---

1. What is my understanding of the principle, "Mind answers to mind"?

2. What are at least six things that my Subjective Mind does?

3. How can I control my health by my thinking?

4. Am I interested enough in good health that I am willing
   to spend from five to twenty minutes a day building it
   for myself?

Your Thinking and Finances

Are you interested in making more money? In running your business more successfully? In getting a better salary? Of course you are! You want to be prosperous, and that is only right and sensible.

The plain, practical, everyday problem of moneymaking is a definite part of living and the answer to it is summed up in these words: *Prosperity awaits our recognition and acceptance of it.* Or this idea can be stated another way: Your financial success already exists, but awaits your seeing it and accepting it as your own.

So far in this book, we have discovered that we are surrounded by limitless Mind–Energy–out of which everything is made. Also, we have found that the nature of the Universe is always to take form according to a pattern, through the process of law. Through our belief and conviction we provide patterns for the manifestation of Law. We may often be helped by realizing that the Universe is infinite, that we can always draw on It for any desired good, and that there is no limit to the good which can be manifest. When we say It "awaits our recognition," we mean that as soon as we intellectually understand the nature of the unseen part of our Universe and the way It works, and wholeheartedly believe in It, then we can more effectively use It.

YOU HAVE A BANK ACCOUNT

If someone told you he had deposited a thousand dollars in your name at a certain bank, but you did not believe him, the money would do you no good even though you were in great need. The money could lie there, idle and useless, even though you starved to death. Even if you *did* believe it but did nothing to make use of it, the money still would do you no good. In order for you to benefit from having the money, you would need to go to the bank and begin drawing on that account. So it is with this principle we desire to use, for not even your intelligent understanding of the accessibility and the limitless nature of infinite Creativity will be of any advantage to you *unless you make proper use of it.*

Learn to draw on your spiritual bank account! Please keep clearly in mind that it is spiritual . . . that everything–including money–is Spirit, Mind, God . . . either visible or invisible. Remember the vapor which changed to ice? The material world is like that. Every tangible thing you see, possess or contact in any way is but an expression of Spirit, manifesting according to a pattern.

If you want more money, you merely need to place your order in this Cosmic Storehouse to have a greater supply of good become tangible in your experience. It is important for you to *identify* yourself with that greater financial supply which you desire, and you cannot do this by thinking about it as though it were impossible or unlikely, or regretting that you do not now have it. Instead, you must train yourself to think about it with a feeling that, reasonably and naturally, it already *is* yours! The money in the bank is yours even though you may not have checked on it yet; you do not have to stop and argue with yourself about its value or accessibility. Likewise, the essence of the All-surrounding Universal Mind is available to you and becomes your experience according to the pattern you choose. If you choose money, then money you will have!

BELIEVE YOUR GOOD IS AVAILABLE

It would be well worth your while to devote some time in your regular routine to get yourself into a mental state of *real* belief in regard to this spiritual bank account of yours. Just as soon as you truly *believe* and *feel* with your whole being that your good is available—when you accept it and know it is yours—then it *is* yours!

When you believe something good is yours, the Universe has no choice but to respond to that belief. This involves a process of identification, by which you not only believe in your financial welfare, but you also act as though it is *now* yours.

When you have a good bank account you certainly are not going to act impoverished. Of course not! You will think, appear and act *prosperous*. Your every attitude will indicate that you are financially successful, for you have identified yourself with prosperity. Anyone who sees you will immediately get this impression. Surely, then, you can begin acting that way *now*, as you realize that you have access to the Universal Storehouse which is limitless.

MAKE YOUR FOUNDATIONS SOLID

To make your financial welfare concrete—that is, to bring it out of the invisible realm of Mind into the visible, tangible realm of your experience—there are certain steps you need to take:

First of all, you must consistently *believe* in its existence. When you actually *expect* it, you are well on the way to meeting it halfway. This form of true expectancy is the highest test of faith.

Next, you need to know that you have the right and the ability *to declare financial success for yourself*—to accept the Creative Action of Mind in this particular way—and also to know you have practical skills and abilities which can be translated into the things people want and will gladly pay for. Wise people never declare their oncoming good and then sit idly by waiting for it to arrive. They use every bit of their knowledge, initiative and skill—the Action of God in them— to make themselves so useful and valuable that financial rewards automatically flow to them.

Some people may sorely need money and have no place to work where they can earn anything. If this is your case, continue looking about you for opportunities, but do that only as a secondary matter. Your task is to understand the Activity of Mind and your creative use of It. Believe in It, declare into It and accept the answer. Know that your "order" has been received and is being filled. With this firmly implanted in your mind, you will be rightly guided when you look for work, for ways to increase your business, for greater outlets for your skill or for whatever other good you may desire.

EXPRESSION THROUGH SERVICE

If, at the start, you successfully find the employment, new plans or whatever else you may have specifically wanted, then be very sure you fill at least a portion of your time afterward by giving service which will help others. It is necessary that you express yourself in a worthy endeavor, because Life is action, and you must be creative in some respect. You might, in fact, be greatly surprised to find that kind, generous, *free* service may be just the thing to set in motion the activities which will result in a job you need, increased business, or some other financial circumstance you desire.

The same is true in regard to giving money. It returns with a certainty and promptness that is astounding! There are hundreds of great needs in the world today where every dollar you can spare will serve some worthy purpose. You should not give carelessly, but when you know of a truly fine work which is being carried on and which needs your support, you do yourself an injustice if you do not contribute to it.

Whether the amount of cash you have is large or small, what you give to others will seem temporarily to deplete your supply—to leave a vacuum. And to say "nature abhors a vacuum" may be trite, but it is a vitally important principle in this connection. When you give intelligently and generously from what you have, for the good of others, you may be absolutely certain that *there will be a spiritual response, and concrete good will come rushing back to fill that empty space!*

A RICH CONSCIOUSNESS

Whether your funds be great or small, you need to get all possible pleasure and satisfaction out of them. This cannot be the case if you fear spending. If you count too carefully, if you limit yourself unduly because you do not know how much money you will have later on, you are restricting your good. If you are going to be rich in concrete ways, you must first be rich in consciousness and have the *feeling* of abundance.

You should let common sense guide your expenditures at all times, but get all the happiness and satisfaction you can out of every dollar you spend. If you are paying rent, buying clothes or food–anything–you are using your money to get something you would rather have than that money, or else you would not use it in that way. Be glad about what you're doing! Never, never hand over your money in payment for anything grudgingly!

If your best judgment suggests a purchase, make the transaction one of mutual goodwill, be it great or small. And the habit of silently blessing your money as you hand it over is worth cultivating, for then it carries with it an intangible value which will bring good things back to you. Learn to bless your bills as you pay them; they indicate the good you have received, and they express the faith others have in you.

WISH GREATLY FOR YOURSELF

You may desire to use money for some particular purpose, but wonder if it is right to do so. "Am I selfish in using my money for this?" you ask. Use this test: "Will it be of value to me, and because of it will I be of greater help, inspiration, encouragement or practical help to others? If so, it is right. If, through me, a greater good can come to others, this money will be wisely spent." If you wish to spend money on something that will start you in a new and worthy service, even though you are using your last dollar, use it wisely, freely and happily.

To bravely step out and do what you can . . . with calm

faith, having made your claim on Universal Creativity, and then with intelligent action as a follow-up . . . will bring the financial abundance you desire.

YOUR RIGHT TO SUCCESS

The Science of Mind teaches a way of thinking which gives you an awareness of spiritual principles on which you may rely. Science of Mind shows you how to use the Law of Mind, how to think effectively (to pray affirmatively) for what you need, so your life becomes wholesome, successful and good. It teaches that your prayers are always answered if they are declared in sincerity, believed in and acted upon by you with common sense and practicality. It declares that you have a perfect right to use the creativity of your mind to provide abundant finances for a fuller, richer experience in living.

WHAT HAVE YOU DONE?

Are you eager for success? Then ask yourself very candidly, "What have I done to earn it? Have I put my very best efforts into my work? Have I developed something new and unique in the service I offer or the business I'm in? Have I made myself especially proficient in one particular field, and am I capitalizing on it? Do I honestly try to think how best to meet the needs of those with whom I do business, so they are most benefited? Can I see things from their viewpoint and adapt myself? Am I constantly improving my skills, my methods and my personality? *What have I done to earn my desired success?*"

In his parable of the talents, Jesus made plain the necessity of using what we possess. A man gave to one servant five talents; to another, two; and to another, one. On his return he called for the money and a report as to how it had been used. It must have been with considerable pride and satisfaction that the five-talent man could report he had doubled his money! So had the man with the two talents. They had used good judgment and worked energetically. They had not wasted time by idly wishing more money were theirs, but had utilized their energies to a good purpose. And so they had passed the test and were given positions of great honor and responsibility; they had proved their initiative, willingness, reliability and business acumen. But the man who made no practical use of what he had—his one talent—found, upon the master's return, that even that one was taken from him. It is a good lesson for all of us to consider. Ask yourself again, "What have I done to earn my success?"

To achieve your desired prosperity, you must:

First, understand that there is an Unlimited Supply which surrounds you; know you have a right to draw on It; believe in the response It always gives; and then *believingly* state your desire and accept the answer. This enables you to get rid of all anxiety about money and supply.

Second, whatever action you take must be taken enthusiastically and energetically. This is your part in bringing about your prosperity. When you have declared your good, you must not try to figure out *how* it is to come. That is for Universal Mind to decide, and It is entirely capable of doing so. Never question *how*; just *know* It does and that It works intelligently.

Remember:

1. Recognize the truth that Universal Abundance surrounds you.

2. Understand and believe in the intelligent, creative responsiveness of the One Mind.

3. Recognize your right and ability to speak your word, believingly, and know that the Activity of Mind, as Law, will manifest the good you choose.

4. Declare your good and know it is made manifest. Let there be no doubt or worry.

5. Act in every practical way you can to bring your prosperity into being.

ESTABLISHING FOUNDATIONS FOR PROSPERITY

I am prospered because I believe in my prosperity.

I accept the responsiveness of the Universe.

The more you make such statements, sincerely believing in them, cultivating a feeling of joy and accepting them as true . . . knowing your perfect right to do so and realizing that Universal Mind is bringing them to pass, the more fully you will establish the foundation for the prosperity you desire.

QUESTIONS FOR SELF-STUDY AND GREATER FOCUS

1. Knowing that "Cosmic" means "Universal," what do you understand by the expression, "Cosmic Raw Material"? The answer should be clear and explicit.

2. Can you put into thirty words what is meant by "Prosperity awaits our recognition and acceptance of it"?

3. Did you ever test the idea of giving freely when you were short of money? What was the result?

4. Do you understand that the good you claim is really yours just as soon as you get a *feeling* it is, even though you cannot see any way it may actually come to you?

5. Is it now plain to you that you really can command financial success through the right use of your mind and appropriate activity?

Rebuilding
Your Life

I t is time to consider a larger concept and to attain a higher spiritual understanding of what you have read so far. You have learned something about what we may call the structure of Universal Mind, and of your relationship to It. You have caught a glimpse of how to make use of that knowledge to bring about good health and financial success for yourself.

However, there is a great spiritual Law which applies to a vastly wider range of subjects and which can apply to everything in life. One way it may be stated is: *We, as children of God, inherit the qualities and powers of the Father.*

To substantiate this we have the words of Jesus: ". . . for one is your Father, which is in heaven." ". . . and all ye are brethren." "For as the Father hath life in himself, so hath he given to the Son to have life in himself." Further confirmation is found in many other religions, in the opinions of philosophers, as well as in the conclusions of many modern scientists.

THE LADDER OF CONSCIOUSNESS

Through eons of time life has been slowly climbing up the ladder of unfoldment to the present self-conscious state achieved in humankind. Some degree of consciousness exists in everything because everything is some form of Spirit, and Spirit is Intelligence. However, there are *degrees* of intelligence, or consciousness. We often hear the expression, "Consciousness sleeps in mineral life, dreams in plant life, awakens in animal life, and comes to self-consciousness in human life."

We, then, stand at the very peak of the evolutionary climb. We are now self-conscious individuals, which means that we not only know, but *know* that we know. We can think about our own consciousness, and we now have the power of choice—the very summit of life's upward striving. Evolution, through infinite ages, has done much for us.

Now, however, if individuals are to continue to progress, we must take things in our own hands and *choose* to continue our climb. From now on, we ascend because we ourselves have chosen to do so. In order to do this, we must clearly realize that there is no separation between humankind and God. Remember, *everything is Spirit*, an expression of the infinite God Consciousness. There is nothing in the Universe that can hinder your upward climb, your increased awareness of Oneness with God . . . unless you decide to stop climbing. The vast expanse of an ever-widening upward reach is available to you.

DESIRE AND WORK FOR THE BEST

In order to promote such growth, you need to recognize the highest qualities in the range of human understanding and you must cultivate them. Because all of us are sons and daughters of God, it stands to reason that each of us has inherited the Father's qualities—and they already lie within us, waiting to be recognized and developed.

Your own logical reasoning makes it plain that if you are to live a highly successful and happy life, you need to be able to *express* those innate abilities, which will in turn produce experiences and conditions of success and happiness.

If those God-given abilities are to be specifically used by you, you need to know about their nature and source. The statement of Jesus that "the Father's life is in the son" surely implies that the son must grow into the qualities of the Father in order to avail himself of that greater potential. You want to live wholesomely, successfully and have a worthy place in the world. If you are to do so you need to get acquainted with the characteristics that make up that kind of life, and then get to work and cultivate them.

YOUR INNER DIVINITY

Each one of us might think of ourselves as an outlet through which the activity of Spirit may flow. In fact, it is only as the qualities of God *do* flow through us that we more fully partake of God's Nature. And that, after all, is our task—to more fully express the Nature of God, the Father. In whatever degree the qualities of perfection are part of our general conduct, to just that degree are we making God known to mankind. We are being true to our sonship only insofar as our inheritance of the Father's Nature is portrayed by us. Each of us has the privilege and the responsibility of being a clear channel for the flow of God through us, as us.

What, then, are these qualities which must be ours? Read
this list and consider it carefully:

> Life
> Love
> Wisdom
> Intelligence
> Peace
> Creativity
> Beauty
> Joy

Unless all of these are experienced fully in your life, you
need to become *more aware* of your unity with God. The
God-qualities are an integral part of you; they lie deep within
you, whether you admit it or not. At the center of your being
are Life, Love, Wisdom, Intelligence, Peace, Creativity,
Beauty and Joy. Immediately you realize that if *all* persons
made use of these qualities—actually lived them—there could
be no inharmony, no lack, no ignorance, no illness, no sor-
didness, fear or sadness.

Growth into our Godlike nature was proclaimed by Jesus
to be "the way, the truth, and the life." It is to this high consciousness that we aspire, and as it unfolds within us, these
qualities are developed. What Jesus did, we too must do. We
have no reason not to fully believe and accept his amazing
statement: ". . . the works that I do shall he do also; and
greater works than these shall he do. . . ."

You honestly do want to accomplish and achieve whatever
will produce for you the wholesome, happy and successful
life—the joyous, healthy life—which your awareness of the
Nature of God holds out for you. To attain these things, you
must recognize that you have, *by nature*, the ability within yourself to attain them. And then you must *cultivate* those parts of
your nature which will let these qualities develop in you.

YOUR INFINITE POSSIBILITY

The first step for you to take involves becoming aware that you *already have* the God-qualities you wish to cultivate and experience in everyday life! This truth is so important and astonishing that you may not grasp its full significance at first. *You already have what you want!* As a child of God you automatically partake of His characteristics. You are part of That which created you. It is your heritage. The qualities of the Nature of God, the Father, constitute perfection, and you are born with them; you were created "in the image and likeness of God."

It may take a good deal of thinking to get this settled in your mind, but when it is, you will find that a big problem in your upward climb is overcome. It is a marvelous revelation to be able to grasp the significance of this magnificent truth—that you already possess Godlike qualities because they are your inheritance. *God is what you are.*

So far these qualities may not have been showing up in your life very clearly, but they are there. So your task now is to *consciously* bring these inner qualities forth, so they can be expressed, used and experienced. You may not have been very good at it previously. Perhaps you have had negative habits of thinking, feeling and acting which kept blocking the right and full expression through you of your Divine nature. If this has been so, do not now concentrate your attention on what you want to get rid of. Instead, devote your efforts primarily to the development of the good qualities you already possess, but have not been using.

THINK ONLY OF YOUR GOAL

The quick and effective way to eliminate anything you don't want is to disregard it and turn your attention and interest to what is directly opposite.

The first of the Godlike qualities listed is Life. You may not have been a very good example of the perfect Life of God. You may have been ill; right now you may think of yourself as being in a run-down physical condition. If there is something you know you ought to be doing in an objective way to build up your health, do it, since "God helps those who help themselves." But the main work lies in your *thinking*. Instead of thinking illness or weakness, think life—Life!

Take time to think about what most fully represents exultant and joyous life—life so full of the sheer joy of living that it cannot be still! Young colts frisking in the pasture, kittens at play, children bubbling with energy! Think of them! *Convince* yourself and know that Life fills your whole body. Know that you not only *have* life, but you *are* Life! Dwell upon this thought, rejoice in it, declare it, give thanks for it, and accept Life as yours right now.

Start expressing It in any and every way you can. Your life is the Life of God within you. Keep affirming this continuously. Accept your physical wholeness as the Perfection of God in you. Be happy about It and know that more and more, It makes Itself manifest in your body.

DO NOT BELITTLE YOUR DIVINE HERITAGE

Remember, you are God's creation; God's Life is your life. Do not belittle that heritage!

You may need to cultivate the quality of Love more than

any of the others. Recall the words of Jesus: "For one is your Father and all ye are brethren." When you stop to really consider this truth—that God is your spiritual Father and that all others are your brothers and sisters—there cannot be any foundation for antagonism toward anyone, since God is not divided against Himself. This leaves the way open for loving thoughts about others and about yourself.

You are a child of God and therefore you should have a very high opinion of yourself; no foolish self-conceit, but reverent understanding of your wondrous relationship to God. Tell yourself over and over again that the quality of Love lies *within* you and that, naturally, you should be expressing It. Think first of those whom you love because of their nearness and dearness to you. Dwell upon their good qualities. Think of those people by name and specify some admirable traits they possess. Kindle within your emotions a warm glow of feeling about them.

Now remember that all *other* people are just as truly worthy of your love, and are in need of it if they are to expand into finer and more beautiful ways of living. They need your love! Spend a few minutes with thoughts of love for all the world (which is sorely in need of every bit of help you can furnish). This is not mere idle wishing. It is a definite service you can render. Your thoughts of love to mankind carry a blessing to the far corners of the globe. Do not neglect to exercise this privilege.

YOU HAVE ACCESS TO THE WISDOM OF GOD

You surely wish at times that you had a greater supply of wisdom-intelligence! But you already have it! Sit quietly by yourself and *know* that as God's child your wisdom is unlimited. Believingly, know that Universal Spirit, All-Wisdom, is now making known to you everything *you* need to know for right decisions, correct choices, proper plans. You need to convince yourself, again and again, that infinite Wisdom is yours to use as you choose. Know that It responds immediately to your every need. Believe it. Joyously accept it. Continue to assert this, and your way will be made plain to you.

Do you feel that you are out of harmony with any person or situation? Is there resentment in your thinking? Do any signs of jealousy or envy gnaw away inside you? Are you fearful or worried about something? If any of these problems are disturbing you, you need but turn your attention to the fact that God can only be Peace and Harmony. Let go of all the tenseness in your body, forget all the mean feelings you may have, and let your body, emotions and mind rest in a deep awareness of that Peace which is God. Be still . . . still in every way . . . and accept the Peace of God, knowing It now heals everything within you that hurts, and that Its calming action enfolds all your experience. Think Peace, feel Peace. Know that you *are* Peace, because you are a definite, specific expression of God, manifesting as you.

CREATIVITY AT THE CENTER OF YOU

Because Life—as Love, Wisdom and Peace—functions through your thinking, there is nothing to hinder Its Creative Action in and through you. God, the Father, has given all power to you—the child. When you recognize and express the Godlike qualities you have always possessed, you can use them creatively for a better life. Beauty and Joy, for example, are two of Life's greatest attributes. Beauty starts to shine through your life as you *think* Beauty, and it makes Itself manifest because It flows from and is inherent in the other Godlike qualities. Life, both inner and outer, becomes so enriched that Joy will permeate your whole being. You *experience* all these qualities, not by searching for them, but by recognizing them deep within yourself; they are your inheritance. Live these qualities. Declare your good, believe in it, and act accordingly. Then you achieve the worthwhile life.

You will not accomplish all of this in one week, for it involves reeducating yourself, and that takes time. But you have made a start. The results will encourage you to continue steadily. Others will see a change in you much sooner than you will realize it yourself. So don't analyze yourself too closely; just go ahead and grow. Your acceptance and expression of the One Life will ever expand.

By such simple procedures as these, men and women have been lifted out of unhappiness, illness, poverty, inharmony and unemployment, into wholesome, productive and highly successful living. These are definite, scientific and spiritual techniques. Follow them if you would move into that glorious realm which awaits those who *choose to attain* and who act accordingly. *As He is so are we, in this world.*

QUESTIONS FOR SELF-STUDY AND GREATER FOCUS

1. Do you understand how self-consciousness, with its power of choice, puts the responsibility for your further progress on you? Explain.

2. Are you making a sincere effort to realize the God-qualities within yourself and to reproduce them in your daily life ?

3. What are two or three occasions during the last week when you put happy emotions into action? What were the results?

You're in Charge!

The old Greek advice, "Know thyself," is profoundly significant to us all. In fact, we *must* know ourselves more fully if we are to lead the successful, happy and useful lives we desire. We see that knowing ourselves better involves understanding our spiritual nature; and also understanding the interrelationship of our mind, body and emotions so we can control them wisely and direct them for our own welfare.

WHO ARE YOU?

All is Spirit. Spirit is Mind. Mind is One. There is no separation between God and you except to the degree you *think* you are separated. If you believe you are locked in a room, and believe it so firmly that you do not even try the doors and windows, the results are exactly the same as though you *were* locked in—though the truth may be that there is no lock and you are free to go as you please. Your *belief* is all that lies between you and freedom. Likewise, you need to banish forever any belief that there is a barrier between God and you. You are *in* God-Mind; you are *of* God-Mind; you *are* God-Mind made manifest in human form.

So you want to be sure that your thinking is not in conflict with itself, and that you have clear, concise thoughts about your true nature. The Science of Mind teaches you to understand your true nature, so you *can* live happily, successfully and with good health, and gradually grow in your expression of God within you. Whatever will tend toward these results should claim your attention. This, in fact, is the kind of practical spiritual thinking you want to learn how to do. Thus, you are ready for the next step: *consciously directing your thought so right and good results are constantly being brought forth in your life.*

THE IMPORTANCE OF HABITS

Let us start with *knowing yourself,* and see if we can find a new way of thinking which will create better results in your life than the old ways.

We have found that infinite Mind, as Law, creates and sustains all things, and so is of prime importance to us. The Law also acts on those persistent thought patterns which have become habits. Every day, therefore, we should add to those habits which are desirable, now that we know how to do it and how they work.

You can add to your supply of good habits by cultivating cheerfulness. It is one of the most helpful traits anyone can have. Thankfulness is another. When we think of how much we have for which to be thankful, it would seem that every moment should be filled with gratitude. A happy expectancy of good is also something to which more attention should be given, until it becomes a fixed habit. You can think of many others, but unless you are really *developing* such habits you are not taking advantage of that exceedingly valuable aspect of the Law of Mind which is always ready and willing to accept whatever you insist upon, sustaining it as a habit which then will function without your having to think about it consciously.

NOTHING IS FORGOTTEN

In this process of knowing yourself, you find that Mind in Its operation as Law—in Its subjective nature—has another characteristic to which you must give attention. It is also the storehouse of memories of former experiences. You may think you have forgotten most of the trivial incidents of childhood (though some few remain vivid in your memory). But thousands of events, acts, circumstances, influences and experiences—of your whole life, including childhood—*are stored away in the subjective part of your mind.* In very large measure they color your life today. Many of them have helped form your attitudes of happiness, courage, self-reliance, hope, faith, initiative, industry and all the other good qualities you have. Here also are stored the memories which may cause many troublesome experiences you encounter.

YOU AREN'T REALLY YOUR MEMORIES

You are usually not able to look back into your life and determine exactly what made a certain impression on you and led to the development of positive qualities you now possess. Really, the total of many individual impressions makes up those good qualities. The same is true in regard to negative qualities. A person really does not usually know precisely how he or she came to have certain attitudes, thought habits or ways of reacting to certain conditions. Irritability, lack of poise, or other negative character traits all seem to be "a part of" yourself. In many cases you do not even know you have such characteristics.

"Why, that's just my nature. I've always been like that!" you may exclaim if your attention is called to certain ways you react to what affects you unpleasantly. And you are honest in saying this. But this isn't your *real* nature, for *you are made in the image and likeness of God.* Therefore, in principle, you are perfect. You could not be otherwise, because perfection is your birthright.

What you *really* are is Life, Love, Wisdom, Intelligence, Peace, Creativity, Beauty and Joy. These are your true characteristics. Anything less is something that has entered your thinking and been placed in subjective mind, where it was acted upon by the Law of Mind, *whether you knew it or not,* and brought into being. So your thoughts, past and present, manifest in your conduct and relationships with others whom you contact.

"But if I don't know what is down there in my mental storehouse, what can I do about it?" you ask, and it is only reasonable that you should. So you first need to realize that there may be undesirable qualities in that storehouse; and second, you must learn how to clean them out.

You no doubt can readily recall a number of incidents which left a scar on your thinking–things you don't forget, which continue to tinge your outlook. And for each one you do remember, probably dozens more have entirely faded from consciousness. Still they are there, steadily influencing or creating your total experience in life.

What to do about them? That's the question!

GIVE THE LAW NEW INSTRUCTIONS

Remember that one very important trait of Mind in Its action as Law is *obedience*; It creates without question. It responds to your firm convictions and beliefs. This should settle any question about how to clean out unwanted thoughts, because now you know that your thoughts of good, acting as a command and a directive, *clean out from that storehouse everything negative and detrimental to your well-being.* This does not mean you must refresh your memory of old influences and events which did you harm. There is no need to know all about them or to review them, but you do want to get rid of them because you cannot afford any longer to harbor anything injurious.

When you make an affirmative declaration, know perfectly well that it will be fulfilled, then keep your conscious thought free of doubts or wondering *how* it should be done, or when. Otherwise you will be hindering the production of the desired results. (It is also productive to declare your good when you are not thinking of a thousand other things. Then the Law of Mind will have a clear and concise pattern for Its action.)

There is no one without some negative ideas and concepts stored away in his or her subjective mind, though he or she is probably totally unaware of many of them. Would it not, then, be wise for *you* to declare affirmatively, day and night, for as long as necessary, that the highly important work of cleaning out the storehouse is now being done? Suppose in six months you could banish the emotional and mental rubbish that has been accumulating there for years and years! Wouldn't that be about the most important thing you could do?

ELIMINATE OBJECTIONABLE HABITS

During the day and as you are about to fall asleep, think of all the positive and desirable character traits you can, whether you are now expressing them in your life or not. Then declare that all which is contrary to them is cleared out, and that only the positive and desirable traits are being established as your experience by the creative action of your thought. *Know* that they fill your whole life and being. Be confident and happy in the knowledge that it is entirely within your right, power, and ability to discard and remove the wrong thought patterns of the past. Get a thorough job of cleaning done, and you immediately start to fill your whole experience with what is Godlike!

Continuously, day and night, this willing, powerful, obedient servant, the Law of Mind, busily fulfills your orders—your *believing* thought. Soon, you can begin to see the difference in yourself; others may see it even before you do. Your whole mental and emotional attitude will change. You will become a new person, completely made over by the Creative Action of God within you.

YOU ARE NEVER A FAILURE UNLESS YOU ADMIT IT

Some old negative patterns of thought have no doubt resulted in frustration. They have made you feel that, at least in regard to some of your great desires, you are a failure. You may have been stopped in every endeavor along certain lines; you may have become bitter in regard to such matters. Now all of this can disappear from your life! You now know that all things are possible.

Perhaps you even see that the very disappointments you

met forced you into something better, or that you can now use them as steppingstones to greater accomplishments. Perhaps some of the experiences of the past hurt you cruelly; your emotional nature was deeply, deeply injured and you thought you would never forget that event! Well, it doesn't matter whether you have forgotten it or not. It is now healed and rendered ineffective, for you have insisted, declared, demanded and accepted that all negatives be cleared away; the obedient, willing, powerful action of God-Mind within you has done it. Although you may feel you have been talking only to yourself, remember that *all Mind is one*, and you really have been turning this matter over to the action of Universal Mind. That is why the results are so sure and so satisfactory.

INFERIORITY IS NO PART OF YOU

You may never have admitted that you felt inferior to others, but there probably have been times when you were timid, shy, reluctant or fearful about attempting something. These are evidences of a thought pattern deep within you which silently suggested that you were inferior. And you accepted that suggestion even if you didn't put it into words. So let's give the matter a little more attention.

We are trying to follow the old Greek adage: "Know thyself." To truly know yourself is to realize deeply, sincerely and constantly that you are made in the image and likeness of God. Therefore, all Godlike qualities are inherent in you. How, then, can you be inferior to anyone? It is impossible! You not only have but you *are* Life, Love, Wisdom, Intelligence, Peace, Creativity, Beauty and Joy. If any previous experiences have made you feel otherwise, know that whatever they are, memories of them are *now* being cleansed, and from now on you are asserting your dominion over any negative thinking which would keep you from your greater good. Reason it out and come to know that *absolutely nothing can deny God in you.* Your conscious mind, however, must back up this process with complete cooperation in every thought— the continual implanting of affirmative ideas of good. This is how you put the Law to work in the *right way*, every day and every night.

EMPHASIZE LOVE AND RIGHTEOUSNESS

You automatically get rid of negatives by implanting positives. Negatives cannot exist when positives fill the space. When the sunshine of love and confidence fills your whole being, the darkness of the negatives has to disappear.

Your emotional nature—the feeling level—is what decides your conduct. The heart is the symbol of the deepest emotions, so whatever you are *at heart*, whether you recognize it or not, is the key to what you really are. "For as [a man] thinketh in his heart, so is he" is from the Bible, but it is also a scientific law, which you should use daily. Reconstruction has to begin in your heart—your feeling nature. This is why a cleansing of negative habits and memories is of primary importance. There must be a reeducation of your emotional reactions.

One of the first requisites of a happy and successful life, for instance, is good health. You cannot be healthy if you harbor *enemies* of wholeness: resentment, fear, self-centeredness and feelings of guilt. Psychologists and physicians say these are the four great enemies of human personality. To banish them, do not focus your attention on them; instead, emphasize their opposites, those characteristics which Jesus urged: Love, Faith, Unselfishness and Moral Rightness.

W. P. Newsholme, in *Health, Disease and Integration,* says: "Hate is poison, not only moral and spiritual poison, but mental and physical poison, as well."

Dr. E. Stanley Jones cites the following incident: "At the close of a meeting, a lady came to me and in a frightened voice said, 'Well, if anger may produce a stomach ulcer, I'm never going to get angry again!'

"She wouldn't listen when 'Thou shalt not hate' was written in the Bible, but she sat up and took notice when she found it was written also in her own stomach."

Simple ideas and rules will help you use the principles of Science of Mind for peace of mind, health of body and buoyancy of spirit! These three aspects of our nature are so closely interrelated that what affects one part has a very definite bearing on all other parts.

You can build bodily health by being emotionally healthy, happy, enthusiastic, hopeful. As you stimulate concepts of spiritual wholeness, you intensify joyous emotional activity. Know that the good cheer, the happiness and the joyous expectancy you are building up in consciousness is being reflected in your health, your financial success and in your ability to live a fuller and more abundant life. *You determine your own welfare!*

QUESTIONS FOR SELF-STUDY AND GREATER FOCUS

1. In the light of what this chapter teaches, write about fifty words on the importance of following the advice, "Know thyself."

2. Write a list of six negative qualities, and directly opposite each, write the one which ought to be cultivated to take its place. (Example: Hate . . . Love)

3. Write six examples of how best to speak to the subjective mind-level to command it to do cleansing work.

4. Write the statement: "As a man thinketh in his heart, so is he," in different, more contemporary words, which have the same meaning.

6 The Power of Directed Emotions

The special attribute which self-consciousness gives us is the *power of choice*. This is certainly a supreme gift of God to humanity. It enables men and women to choose their own destiny—accepting Divine Wisdom and Power in such ways that they can have their chosen destiny become actual experience.

It is true, however, that every privilege brings its corresponding responsibility. The right and power to make your own decisions, bad ones or good ones, puts you in a very sensitive position. You now realize you are no longer an automaton, moved about by the caprice of circumstance, solely guided by instincts, or subject to some will superimposed on you. You are free to choose! But you have to take the consequences of that choosing.

The universal creative Law of Mind, of which your actions are a part, creates for you according to your choice. Too often that choice is prompted by unwise, impetuous emotional attitudes, without due regard to thoughtful decision. Too often, a negative emotional reaction directs your decisions rather than the process of logical thinking—that ability of the conscious mind which enables you to think things out clearly and to decide accordingly. Thus, you need to take clear and certain responsibility for what you create with your attitudes.

EVERYTHING ACCORDING TO LAW

What you are deeply *feeling* is usually what you are establishing in Mind as cause; it is the pattern for what you will receive.

To make this more clear—even though you may have thought of this illustration before—think about the soil in the garden. When you wish to produce a crop of any kind you first prepare the soil, using your best knowledge to get it into the right condition so it will bring forth what you want to grow. When the earth is well prepared, free from obstructions, properly fertilized and made ready in every way to receive the seed; when the rain and the sun have done their part and you have carefully selected your seeds and made your plans, then you begin the planting. You plant *only* those seeds that will grow into what you want in your garden. You may want a row of radishes in between one of beets and one of carrots. Close by in the same soil, you plant cabbages; then next, perhaps watermelons.

From the good, reliable, dependable soil, the radish seed draws whatever is needed to produce white radishes with red skins. But, *from exactly the same soil* in the very next row, you get carrots, bright orange-yellow all the way through and tasting not one bit like the radishes. And on the other side are deep red beets of still another texture and taste. All the other kinds of seeds bring forth according to their own nature and—*this is the point*—you knew they would! That is why you planted them. No one is wise enough to pick out of the soil the chemicals to produce the different results, but then no one has to.

So, your part is fourfold: Get the soil ready, choose the right seeds, plant them and give the garden the right care and attention. The marvelously wise soil of Mother Nature takes charge of the processes of production.

No one can explain how or why this happens. But just because of lack of such understanding, do we fail to take advantage of it? No. Year after year, millions of men and women plant gardens and know in advance what harvest they are going to have.

In the spiritual realm, Universal Subjective Mind as Law is the soil. It is just as dependable, just as reliable, and functions just as naturally as the soil in the garden. It takes whatever you choose to plant in It, and produces accordingly. You, personally, are the one who determines what kind of results you are going to have. That is one of the principles you need to keep constantly in mind.

Whatever you decide with your conscious mind and then commit to the action of the Law, in quiet trust and in perfect confidence, will come to pass for you. No one knows just *how* thoughts become concrete and tangible; neither does anyone know how one part of the soil produces a carrot when the very same soil, only a few inches away, brings forth a luscious watermelon. But just because the action is not completely understood, has this kept people from planting seeds?

Of course not! Likewise you can be equally trustful about your spiritual planting.

CAREFUL PREPARATION

Care was used in preparing the garden soil in order to get it into the proper condition. Here again the analogy to spiritual processes is true: We must remove from the creative medium of Mind all negatives. It must be at peace. Everything must be removed that would obstruct the right development of whatever good results we seek. When you are poised, calm, at peace, filled with happy expectancy and serenely trusting in the fulfillment of the highest good, you are ready to do your spiritual planting.

All summer long the warmth of the sun and the refreshment of gentle rains bring your garden through the various stages of growth to rich maturity, which is the reason you planted it. Your spiritual garden, first planted in the soil of emotional serenity, must be kept nourished with love and watered with expectancy. Do not let any weeds of doubt or anxiety hinder its progress. Give it daily attention, entirely free from worry or fear as to the outcome. Remember, you can trust the soil to do its part *if you do your part!*

CAREFUL PLANTING

In your spiritual garden, you are always planting something—desires, longings and hopes . . . or fears and worries. There is no special season set aside for this kind of planting. Therefore, the subjective-mind soil must be in the right condition all the time. You are always planting, and you cannot afford to have the good seeds dropped into soil that contains a mass of weeds. You cannot afford to plant bad seeds—

thoughts of negation, worries, fears, angers, hates, resentments. Such seeds will grow just as rapidly as the good seeds and will bring forth a crop of problems, just as surely and abundantly. The soil of the garden has no power or inclination to reject bad seeds while accepting good ones. Similarly, your subjective-mind level, the creative medium of Law, also is entirely impersonal and will just as readily take your negations and produce for you a crop of illness, poverty, hardship, difficulty or inharmony. So be careful about your planting!

When you first start getting your garden ready you are likely to find that it contains a good many stones, weeds, hard chunks of earth or rubbish. These need to be cleaned away if the soil is to produce as you desire. Similarly, old complexes, attitudes and habits certainly will ruin your harvest in the spiritual realm unless you get them out.

One thing that often has to be removed is a sense of inferiority. All you really need to get rid of it is the realization that you are God's child; God is what you are. So, you are inferior to no one! Some may be more talented along certain lines than you, but deep within each person lies the very same Life, expressing in an individual manner—through particular talents and abilities. You are made in the image and likeness of God, and therefore you *cannot* be inferior to anyone in the world!

A superiority complex is also a type of weed no one wants flourishing in his or her garden. It is also removed by realizing that all of us are God's children and are filled with His qualities; that *each* of us is a superior expression of Life and expresses that Life according to our nature.

To bring about continuous unfoldment and the accomplishment of desired results, get your garden cleaned up. Then do the right kind of planting.

FORGIVE YOURSELF

Even though you may not be troubled by what are usually known as inferiority or superiority complexes, you still may have a sense of self-condemnation—a frame of mind which has been referred to as a guilty conscience—which thwarts your efforts toward happiness and success, and keeps you so disturbed that your highest efficiency is impaired. To be out of harmony with oneself in this way is, indeed, a sad condition.

Many people were brought up to be so deeply aware of some sort of critical inner monitor, one which usually accused them of something, that they have had a pretty hard time getting away from it. The sad part is that with a more mature judgment, many have come to know that most of the little things considered "wicked" in childhood are now found to have nothing of evil in them. Early training may have led some to believe that wearing bright colors, for instance, was a sin. To read a story, no matter how high the moral tone, if it was not an actual fact, was evil. These and a hundred other narrow restrictions bind and limit people. Because you were just an ordinary boy or girl, with a natural yearning for what was banned, you may have found some way to wear the forbidden color, or you secretly and guiltily read the book. Ever since then you could have been burdened with a sense of having committed a sin. Such self-condemnation can hang over a person like a cloud, obscuring the outgiving of God's love and the expression of His Nature.

These illustrations may seem very insignificant, but they indicate the problems of many a troubled mind. And even though they may not be active in the conscious mind, they remain active at the subjective level, coloring our attitudes and actions.

A FALSE SENSE OF GUILT

We need to be thankful that an All-wise Father has planted within us a guide to the right conduct which we call conscience! But we also need to be careful that we do not allow it to destroy our happiness because of something which, when seen with correct judgment, has no moral wrongness to it. Dr. Smiley Blanton tells us that "unless the growth of conscience is wisely directed the results will be serious conflict." He adds that the process of conscience-building includes four phases:

1. A primitive impulse of love.

2. A profound need for holding our parents' love and being obedient to them.

3. A synthesis of the child's impulse for self-criticism with the parental criticism.

4. The modification of all these feelings by the contact with life.

The first three of these developmental phases take place in childhood. Then, through all the mature years, much time is spent trying to get rid of a lot that was created in those early, formative years. The sad part, though, is that much of the harm done is never undone. We may outgrow the feeling that parents are watching and blaming us for shortcomings, but we are likely to transfer the same feeling to a deep conviction that God is watching for every misdoing, is blaming us, and that punishment of some kind is being handed out or stored up. Often this goads us on to doing other and much worse "sins." Certainly when we have done wrong we ought to be sorry about it and promptly mend our ways, but wallowing in negative emotions and not doing anything constructive about the matter will do us no good.

The complexes–bad weeds–have to be rooted out of our spiritual garden. And the way to remove a negative is to turn our attention to its opposite–positive good–and cultivate it.

So . . . we know the qualities of God's Nature and we know how to develop them. The conscious mind must learn to sit in the driver's seat and direct what takes place; emotions must be controlled; and if we are to be successful gardeners, we must see to it that the right kind of planting is done. We must learn to rule our own lives. ". . . he that ruleth his spirit [is better] than he that taketh a city."

Even the simplest little device that brings this procedure down from the abstract and puts it into concrete form is exceedingly helpful. Any expedient that tends to make you *feel* that you are taking the right step will have tangible value.

So learn to praise yourself for the qualities you want to develop. Be as kind and encouraging to yourself as you would be to anyone else who was trying to improve. Your whole life–thought, body and emotions–will soon respond to the praise you give it and you will really develop the good qualities desired! Remember, you are always planting something!

QUESTIONS FOR SELF-STUDY AND GREATER FOCUS

1. Write clearly your understanding of the necessity of cleansing your subjective mind.

2. Explain the necessity of following the dictates of conscience, and yet of ridding yourself of false restrictions which you have been holding for years.

3. Describe two ways in which some emotions are of great value in your life, and two ways in which others promote difficulties.

The Personality
of Value

I f there is a type of personality that pays—and there *is*—you naturally want to know more about it. You want to bring it forth in your own life and be in a position to reap the benefits from it.

First of all, what is personality? For many years, philosophers and psychologists have discussed this elusive "something" known as a good personality; they have tried to explain it, they have sought to show its desirability, and how to acquire it. Probably they will continue to do so, and the longer they do the greater will be the number of explanations given.

A definition which seems to meet our requirements at this time is: *Personality is the way a person expresses his or her individuality.* Let us separate this into its key parts and see if we can reveal its true significance.

"Personality . . ." means the characteristics a person displays, the degree to which he or she has developed certain traits and qualities, and the way in which the person shows them forth in his or her life—appearance, speech, actions, attitudes, the way that person appears to the rest of the world.

". . . expresses his or her individuality." Personality is the result of what a person does—his or her thinking, emotions, actions—with what a person actually *is*, his or her individuality. We are all children of God, individualizing all the qualities of God. According to this spiritual heritage, we have every characteristic of our spiritual Father: Life, Love, Wisdom, Intelligence, Peace, Creativity, Beauty and Joy.

WHAT YOU THINK YOU ARE
PROCLAIMS ITSELF

The more you come to realize your true spiritual nature, the more you will be able to let it flow through you and express as your personality; the more you will be able to show to all the world your understanding of Life; the clearer your thoughts will be about your real nature and the more you will be able to experience it.

You are an individual, and you must express that individuality to the fullest extent *as your personality*. To the degree that you fail to recognize or express your individuality, you will deny yourself the experience of the joyous attributes of Life. That which others know you to be through your personality will be good or bad depending upon what *you* know you are. So proclaim yourself with no uncertainty to represent the highest qualities you know God to be.

PERSONALITY ADVANTAGES

Now that you know developing a good personality is truly possible for everyone, let us consider some aspects of personality.

Social. This aspect of personality is probably more important than any other trait you may develop. Those with a good social personality get along well with others; they are always desirable associates.

The simple, easy, sure way to test your own personality in this respect is to ask yourself candidly, "Do people like to have me around?" If they do, you may be sure that your social personality is a pleasing one. Of what value to you is it for them to like having you around? It adds to job security, brings you opportunities for advancement, draws many friends to you, and makes life a happy experience.

Physical. A good personality likely includes good physical health, for health of body is the outpicturing of health of mind. If you accept the Perfection of God indwelling in you, you automatically assure yourself of good health. If there were no other inducement to the cultivation of a good personality, this in itself would be enough.

Financial. The rewards of a Godlike personality are beyond computation. It holds the secret to abundance, insures business and professional success, and opens the way for financial remuneration. Often financial rewards depend to a considerable extent on our ability to bring all of our capabilities to bear on a situation with strong focus. People whose personalities are agreeable, kindly, considerate and tolerant usually meet little or no opposition. They do not ordinarily have to fight for what they know is right (in fact, others easily fall in line with what is good and right). If, temporarily, they need to set aside their own desires, they do so gracefully and in a short time, events and conditions become readjusted. They soon find things going in the right way. A healthy personality is the key to financial success.

Spiritual. Individuals who attune themselves to God are constantly striving to reproduce in their own lives high spiritual qualities, and as a result those qualities daily become more and more fully expressed through their personalities. These people are so deeply interested in being about the "Father's business" that they steadily grow in their ability to reflect the attributes of God.

So, those with well-developed personalities are happy people. Because of their social, physical, financial and spiritual well-being, their happiness is assured. Even in the midst of the varied demands of a busy life, they are ever serene, poised and at peace with themselves, their fellow men and women, and their God.

THE PERSONALITY WORTH CULTIVATING

We arrive, then, at three conclusions concerning the type of personality worth developing.

1. A good personality involves sending forth those God-qualities which lie inherent in you.

2. A good personality enables you to live so your presence is desired—others "like to have you around."

3. This results in your having more advantages than would otherwise be possible. One of these is the opportunity to experience more abundance of all kinds, including money.

SOME INTERESTING ILLUSTRATIONS

During the worst years of the Depression, a group of psychologists from Harvard set out to investigate for themselves the real cause for the layoffs which were so prevalent. They knew that business was exceedingly slow and often did not warrant keeping a full quota of employees, but why were some discharged and others retained? What was the determining factor? If this could be uncovered, it might be helpful to many and enable them to avoid being laid off.

The investigation involved 4,000 men in Boston for a period of a year and represented all classes of workers—unskilled, skilled, professional, clerical and executive—so as to get a general cross-section of the situation.

In every case the facts were secured from both sides—employer and employee.

Here are some of the startling facts that were revealed:

The reports showed that instead of the majority of reasons for dismissal being "poor business," "necessity for curtailing," "reducing overhead" and similar remarks (which the investigators expected to receive), only a small number of those who had been dismissed lost their jobs because of such reasons. When all the figures were compiled, it was found that:

✦ 16 percent had lost their jobs because of inefficiency or distinct lack of ability in their particular work;

✦ 8 percent were out of work because their behavior violated customary standards for personal conduct—in a few cases gross misdemeanors were involved;

✦ 13 percent had been dismissed for miscellaneous reasons, including decreased business for the firm.

✦ 63 percent made up the remainder and all of them had lost their positions in that crucial period, when it was practically impossible to get other employment, *simply because they did not get along well with their associates!*

The survey showed that in one year, in one city, out of 4,000 cases investigated, a total of 2,520 men lost their chance to make a living, not because of not being needed, not for any crime, not because of lack of ability, but simply because their personalities were such that others did not "like to have them around"!

If no other illustrations were ever encountered, this survey should be enough to prove the "money value" of a pleasing personality.

PERSONALITY QUOTIENT

During the past fifty or so years, business and professional men, and especially educators, gave much attention to an individual's "Intelligence Quotient."

"How high is his or her I.Q.?" was often one of the first questions asked when a person was being considered for almost any position. This was done to insure that workers were given jobs which suited themselves and their employers most satisfactorily. However, any good thing can be carried too far; any virtue may become a vice by overemphasis. This may have been the case in regard to the I.Q., for keen, hard-headed employers came to see that a person's I.Q. is not nearly so important as is his or her "P.Q." (Personality Quotient), and this is what they are now insisting upon.

"Do they make friends easily and get along well with the public, as well as with their coworkers? Will they be an asset to the company?"

With this in view, authorities at one of our leading universities decided to make a survey as to the relative merits of the I.Q. and the P.Q. in the experiences of some of their graduates. At Commencement Day one year, a group of one hundred men with brilliant I.Q.'s were listed, without their knowing it, and their careers watched for results. All of them had done remarkably well academically, but had failed to mix with their fellows, probably because of their great interest in studies. They had been the typical introvert types, interested solely in meeting high educational standards and consequently shutting themselves off from their companions.

Another group of one hundred, chosen the same day from the graduating class, consisted of men whose academic standings had been so mediocre that they barely succeeded in passing, but whose genial qualities of personality made them so popular that they were greatly liked by all who knew them. They had probably given of themselves in student activities too freely for the good of their scholastic records, but all through their college careers they had happy and useful associations, and made many friends.

In neither of the two groups did anyone know he was being made the subject of a test.

THE PROOF OF THE PUDDING

Because it usually takes a professional man from five to seven years to get established, as he passes through the so-called "starvation period," the university authorities felt it would not be fair to announce any results until all had ten years in which to prove themselves. This, they felt, would be a reasonable test, and they were eager to see what they could learn as to the value of the much-wanted I.Q.

The group of one hundred was large enough to average

out individual exceptions; it really was a good test. And at the end of the ten years it was found that the salaries of the high P.Q. men were, on the average, over three times greater than the salaries of the men with brilliant I.Q.s!

These P.Q. men liked people; people liked them and liked to have them around. They progressed in their business or profession, led happy lives and made money.

So, to develop a personality that pays—pays in good dollars and cents, in happiness, friendships and health—is something of specific interest to all of us. It is a definite part of our spiritual training. It is one of the steps in that upward climb which takes us into greater spiritual awareness. Such aspiration has its rightful place, for it points the way to wholesome, happy, efficient, Godlike living.

THE HIGH PRIVILEGE OF RIGHT THINKING

How shall we attain such a personality—one that pays? We need to constantly remind ourselves of the Godlike qualities which by nature lie within us, and we must renew our daily, persistent efforts to bring them into manifestation in our lives. The process involves thought and spiritual awareness, but it also needs constantly to be accompanied by those objective activities which translate our high resolves and rich aspirations into action. In our contact with everyone, we must be aware of the necessity and the high privilege of putting all the good, kindly, thoughtful, helpful, encouraging and inspiring qualities we learn into actual practice as we deal with people.

Your thoughts must be right, your motives right, your eagerness to build a Godlike life far more outstanding than a desire to be a good money-maker. "Seek ye first the kingdom of God, and his righteousness, and all these things shall be added unto you," is a statement one cannot afford to ignore.

Your thinking must be right, and you must remember what is said in Philippians: "Whatsoever things are true . . . honest . . . just . . . pure . . . lovely . . . of good report; if there be any virtue, and if there be any praise, think on these things." This is not only good moral advice, but it is psychologically sound, and it is good common sense.

SOME THINGS TO REMEMBER

You have seen the reasons why you ought to cultivate a fine personality; you have seen the advantages of it; common sense tells you to do it. Your privilege and responsibility is to cultivate the "personality that pays." *Be ye transformed by the renewing of your mind.*

So, if there is anything you dislike about your life circumstances, state clearly in one sentence what you *do* want. For example, you might be accustomed to saying, "My work is dull and monotonous, and I do not like my associates." Now change that thought to one which expresses exactly the opposite: "I am steadily finding new interest in my work and pleasing qualities in those about me."

Regardless of what your problem is, do your best to affirm its opposite—that which you want. You may not succeed totally the first day or week, but continue all day and evening for a whole month and see if you don't completely rebuild your attitude in regard to that certain problem. This practice will pay rich rewards.

Also, develop a habit of looking for the good in others and praising them for it.

Think of the qualities you may particularly need in your own special work—alertness, energy, initiative, speed, appearance, faithfulness, poise or cheerfulness. Whatever they are, resolve to improve yourself. You are the only one who can improve your personality, but it is important . . . and anything which helps you do so is valuable. *Be ye transformed by the renewing of your mind,* and you and your affairs will be renewed as you transform your thinking.

QUESTIONS FOR SELF-STUDY AND GREATER FOCUS

---

1. Put into about fifty words your understanding of the statement, "Personality is what a person is—vocalizing itself."

2. Do you mingle with people easily? If so, continue to do so, but never fritter away time uselessly. If it is difficult for you to make friends, decide upon at least one activity you can enjoy—bowling, tennis, hiking or anything that will keep you enjoying yourself physically and actively, preferably out-doors—*with others*. Write a short statement as to what you will do to participate with others in that activity.

QUESTIONS FOR SELF-STUDY AND GREATER FOCUS

3. Carefully observe among your acquaintances one person who evidently has a high P.Q. Decide what his or her special qualities are and write them here.

4. Why is it necessary to be thinking about such things as Philippians tells us to? ("Whatsoever things are true . . ." etc.) What does such thinking do for us?

8

Finding Life's Riches

What a person believes and does, determines the results he or she gets! But some may say, "That is a very good theory, but it doesn't work out in actual life. I've always done the best I could, though things don't go right for me. I'm not one of the lucky ones!"

But we are once again impressed with the fact that the responsibility for what a person experiences is a result of his or her own thinking. This is the direct result of being human, of possessing consciousness—that aspect of human development which gives each one the right and power of choice.

YOU ALONE CHOOSE YOUR GOOD

The primary fact is that we desire greater good—health, money, harmony; better business, greater supply, different and better employment—or anything else which will add to our joy of living.

How does the Science of Mind teach us to get it? Common sense says you first need to understand spiritual Law—that Law which you are attempting to use. You need to remind yourself that Spirit surrounds you and is unlimited, and is the Source of all things; also that It is always *becoming* something in your experience, and the nature of that "something" is decided by you. You must remember that Law is entirely impartial and neutral. It does not care what demand is made upon It. It produces whatever is planted in It, just as does the soil in a garden. Certainly by this time you have that understanding. You know about this spiritual activity even if you do not always use it for your good.

Even if the "garden" illustration is very simple and has already been given repeatedly, remember this important part of it: though you cannot understand the processes in your garden as the seeds develop into plants, you do not have to wait for a complete understanding of this marvelous process of nature; *you just go ahead and make use of it.* This is your guide for right now. What does it matter if you do not see how a thing you desire can actually be? You are after results; that's what counts!

ACCEPT AND USE GOD'S LAW

You know that the radish seed will produce radishes and *nothing else*; and you know that the *only thing* which can grow from your carrot seed is carrots. Because you *know*, you act accordingly. You *accept* this as a law of nature on which you can depend. Let's see now if you can be just as sensible in the matter of your spiritual planting, where you need that same kind of acceptance.

Such acceptance has to involve a deep conviction, a perfect belief. Do not try, by force of will, to compel yourself into this belief. Let go of all striving—God's way of doing things must be the best way. Just say to yourself, "This is the way such things are done. I have learned enough to know that this is God's method of getting results and I accept it. I believe it. I know it is so! Yes, I accept. The particular result to which I am now giving my attention is *already mine*. The great limitless Source of supply is merely waiting for me to place my order. Because I have sufficient understanding of infinite Law to know this is the way my good comes to me, and because I have chosen what it shall be, I am meeting the requirements of the Law, so I *know* this particular good is mine, *now*.

"I *feel* the experience of it. I picture myself enjoying it. I see its desirability and value. I am planning how it adds to my experience of worthy living. Because of what it is to me, or the special ways in which I use this good, I am of greater helpfulness and inspiration to others. This is one of the reasons why I chose it. I know that my main work in life is to 'be about my Father's business,' and this good makes me able to do that more effectively. Whatever I receive is only being entrusted to me as a worthy steward of God's abundance.

"Only as I use talents, privileges, opportunities, responsibilities or funds wisely will they benefit me. I shall not bury them in the ground, I shall not hoard them; I shall *use* them constantly so they serve others. In that service, they shall increase. I produce intelligently and plentifully with what is entrusted to me. The good I have chosen is now mine!"

FAITH UNIFIED WITH WORKS

Now we consider the process of building a "Mental Equivalent." We need to feel that the desired good is actually ours *now*! And it is! This is how the Law works; It manifests what we accept. *This is Faith.*

When this deep consciousness has been reached, it is a good idea to put the specific desire into words and to speak them forth, with perfect assurance of your right and power to do so. This plants the seed in the spiritual soil and it confirms the result in your own consciousness, so you feel a rich and happy satisfaction in knowing you have now done *your* part in the creative sequence. You have prepared the soil, chosen your seed, and planted it. It is now committed to the Creativity of infinite Spirit, which brings forth your crop.

This "declaration" unifies Faith with Works. It is affirmative thought made with spiritual awareness, with understanding and acceptance.

The fundamental thing you have to remember is that this is a spiritual process of making yourself fully receptive; so with an attitude of perfect acceptance, make your declaration. Your mental garden, however, will not be a success unless you tend it. It's going to be real work to have it produce the desired results, but you will not be satisfied with anything less than complete fulfillment.

THE JOY OF RIGHT ACTION

From the Mental Equivalent part of our endeavor we now move to the Right Action part, for there is work to be done. Surely, the first part (establishing the Mental Equivalent) is of prime importance, for unless you had chosen your good and declared it, there would have been nothing from which to expect returns. Still, if you do not give it continuous attention you cannot expect a very significant return, but you will be so thrilled by what you *do* see developing and by the satisfaction that always comes from achievement, that the process will not seem difficult. In fact, it really is a pleasure and you are richly repaid for all you do.

So, the good you have chosen and planted in the realm of Cause requires definite action on your part, and it needs to be Right Action too! "God does *for* us what He does *through* us" is a truth of such importance that we can never afford to ignore it. ("God helps those who help themselves" is but another way of putting it.)

Everything you *can* do objectively to promote this chosen good is, of course, what you *are* going to be doing. Anything less would be childish and infantile. You don't expect to get anything without paying the right price for it. That price, in the objective world, usually consists of good work, systematic study, personal development, or any concrete action that represents your part in the transaction.

When you planted your garden you knew it would require tending all summer. Now you have planted some great, sincere, worthy desire in the realm of Cause, and you must likewise be sincerely willing and eager to do your objective part so it will develop for you. This is Right Action. This is *Works*. *Faith without Works,* as the Bible says, *is dead.*

DECLARE RIGHT ACTION INTO OPERATION

The phrase "Right Action" has a still deeper and slightly different meaning. During your meditation time, when you contemplate what your choice is, when you know it is a worthy one—and particularly when you know it is secondary to the basic one, "Seek ye first the kingdom of God"—you also know that, in most cases, its concrete development will involve activity on the part of other people. Someone may need to participate in a certain way, or the cooperation of several persons may be required, or readjustment may be needed in a situation that now seems to stand in the way of the fulfillment of your desire. Whatever it is, no person is wise enough to know just what and how everything should take place.

You always need to remember that even when you understand a situation thoroughly and have used your very best judgment, when you think you can clearly see conditions, circumstances and results, *finite mind—your individual mind—can see only superficially.* Infinite Mind, however, can see and know all that is underneath, above and around . . . past, present and future . . . all of which is entirely shut off from your limited, conscious vision. The particular adjustment which you think is desirable may not, after all, be the right one. There may be a dozen different aspects of which you know nothing, and all of them may have a definite bearing on the right outcome of this desired good of yours. What, then, can you do? Will you throw up your hands in helpless despair, saying, "What's the use? I don't know what ought to be"?

Not at all! Our mind is a particular expression of God-Mind, through which God's Wisdom, as a creative and directive action, may be brought to bear upon particular situations and circumstances. Such action is always right, because it is God-Action. Therefore, part of your declaration is setting into motion whatever shall be "Right Action" in order that what is best for all will be brought to pass. With perfect assurance, you may declare this Right Action as taking place. Then you are sure of the right results.

DO NOT OUTLINE

Some of your most carefully thought out and diligently executed activities may seem for the moment to fail in promoting your desired good. But do not judge too quickly. What's going on may be just a step toward the fulfillment of those unseen processes which eventually bring to pass what is wanted. No hasty judgment should be made as to the effectiveness or noneffectiveness of what you have done. Back of it all there must be a calm assurance that "Right Action" is manifesting in the events that occur, for you have declared your acceptance of it. Whether the Right Action is taking place as a result of your own efforts, the work of others, or any one of a hundred different events, contacts, influences or circumstances, it does not matter.

You can be certain that what is right is being done. The process involves intellectual understanding of spiritual Law, emotional conviction that the chosen good is truly yours, the oral declaration of it to fasten it firmly in your consciousness, and the final knowledge that it is established as the law of your experience.

There must also be spiritual realization that everything conforms to law and order, and that nothing can keep your good from being developed in the right way and delivered to you. (There always must also be the physical activity on your part which rounds out the procedure. This is the combination of Faith and Works which guarantees success.)

NORMAL GROWTH

About a week or so after you planted your garden, did you come home one afternoon and spend an hour or two working in it? Did you look it over and decide it was a failure because it had not come to maturity? Did you decide that it was all a mistake on your part to think you were going to reap any results? Did you say, "Nothing has come of it. I'll never try that again"? Certainly you did not. You knew it would take time.

It also takes time for you to grow in spiritual knowledge and realize the power of declaration, acceptance and activity. Growth is not instantaneous; it is gradual. Results do not often come immediately. In nearly all cases, the desired results come to pass through normal human agencies. If we need more money, it does not rain down from the sky. It comes to us through natural, normal channels. In practically all cases the fulfillment of our desires is tied up with other people and what they think, say and do. The Right Action you have decreed may prove to be something that involves considerable time, but you have to accept, *right now*, that the desired results are manifest.

When you know deep in your heart that what is right is taking place even though you see no evidence of progress, you surely have no occasion for impatience or disappointment. Happily, expectantly, you go ahead doing what seems wise—energetically and enthusiastically—but free from all stress or strain. Your order has been placed in the Universal Storehouse and there is nothing to be concerned about.

Remember these two points:

1. Your own spiritual awareness is growing.

2. The events, influences and activities that will produce Right Action for you are going through natural processes—which will bring the right result, whether or not you see the steps in the process.

BE REASONABLE

If you had no experience in planting, cultivating and tending crops, it would be foolish to start with a thousand-acre farm of diversified products. It would be better to begin with a few acres while you learned farming principles. Gradually you would get ready for larger ventures later on, with increased assurance and fewer doubts. The same is true in the spiritual realm. It is wise to use this principle first in the small affairs of everyday living; to become skillful you may need lots of practice. The principle is unfailing but you need skill in using it, so don't postpone the positive use of the Law for good until you are faced with a big emergency. Practice today on the small needs.

Surely there isn't a day without its own special requirements—small perhaps, but confronting you *now* and demanding solution. Begin today taking all your hour-by-hour needs and applying the principle of Faith and Works to them. Just such simple matters as these may present themselves:

✦ I want to get that little matter of a neighborhood squabble among the children adjusted.

✦ I need to make more efficient collections of my bills this month.

✦ My place of business needs some better equipment.

✦ How shall I make my advertising bring better results?

✦ Greater harmony in my family and among my workers ought to be brought about.

✦ I need to improve my skill and earn a higher salary.

Keep steadily in mind that faith in this principle is of first importance: Believe, declare, then accept; all of this activates

Universal Mind. Then *you* act accordingly, for this is your work in the objective realm of experience.

QUESTIONS FOR SELF-STUDY AND GREATER FOCUS

1. Name any one desire you might have, then write briefly all the steps you would take in building a Mental Equivalent and in assuring yourself of Right Action in regard to it.

2. Now itemize a number of the things you would do objectively to bring it to pass.

QUESTIONS FOR SELF-STUDY AND GREATER FOCUS

3. During the week, experiment with some small desire. Carefully follow the directions of this chapter and then write a brief record of your experience.

Spiritual Growth

There is something within us all which constantly pushes us forward, which demands our continued progress.

Inertia may hinder our paying much attention, but this inner urge is always there. It is what keeps us going ahead, sometimes almost against our will. An inherent quality in all people, it asserts itself whether we welcome it or not, because it is what *we are*, demanding expression.

Made in the image and likeness of the Father, we cannot accept stagnation; something protests against it. We must move forward into a higher and more satisfying spiritual stature. This "divine discontent" is a factor in our very makeup, and unless we are following its promptings we are not happy. We cannot get away from it because it is a part of our nature. Its activity in us promotes what we call "spiritual growth."

You are probably well aware that many people seem to have disregarded the important matter of spiritual growth, and, insofar as can be seen, they are going down instead of up. But this may be entirely beside the point, because we do not know their inner experiences, their thoughts, hopes or longings. We do not know just where they are in spiritual awareness, nor how much they had to overcome in order to get even that far. Though we may have known them from childhood, still we cannot really know their background in all its details. Because of this we cannot possibly know what their efforts toward growth really are. *It is not our place to judge them.* We have all we can do to look after our own unfoldment, which is something for which we are specifically responsible.

DIFFERENT ASPECTS OF UNFOLDMENT

It is encouraging to realize that your very nature is such as to keep you growing, and also to provide the instrument through which that growth is accomplished. You have a physical body, a complex emotional nature and an intellect. These three aspects of your nature are so closely interrelated and they react so strongly upon each other, that you have a triple set of capacities to utilize in the process of advancement.

You are probably better acquainted with the nature of your physical body than with your emotions and mind, so let us begin with it. The body is the house in which, for the present, you are living and you need to keep it in good repair by a right mental attitude toward it. Your body is entitled to your respect. "Know ye not that your body is the temple of the holy [Spirit] . . . ?"

The body is particularly responsive to your emotional

states. If you are sad, discouraged, gloomy, worried or fearful—all of which are troublesome emotions—your body immediately reflects that troubled feeling and your state of health is lowered. (The word "health" is simply the modern version of the Old English "wholth," meaning wholeness.) If you are not healthy emotionally, you cannot be in good health physically.

AN ATMOSPHERE OF EMOTIONAL HEALTH

We know now there is such a close relationship between the body and the emotions that we seek to build bodily health *through* emotional healing. Time ought to be given daily to such building. It is especially wise to keep faithfully in mind such expressions as these:

"I am filled with the Life and Love of God."
"I feel strong and vibrant."
"God-Life surges through my entire body."
"I function normally, wholesomely and effectively."
"The Power and Perfection of God flow through me constantly and keep me in superb health."
"I rejoice in emotional wholeness."

When such statements are contemplated with real happiness, they carry a thrill of joy to every part of the body. They create and maintain an atmosphere of health, which becomes a part of new cells that are created. The good feeling which attends such statements becomes an attitude in the body and if persisted in, becomes a habit carrying with it the power to continually reproduce itself.

This is very important, because we all sometimes find ourselves below par physically and need something to bring us back to normality. One of the best things you can do is to practice using such assertions, and also to practice having a healthy body, expanded chest, erect posture and free and easy carriage—all of which indicate good physical condition. Merely repeating one of the statements will at once tend to reproduce the associated physical condition. These "automatic reflexes" are wholesome; they cost you nothing in cash; they occupy only a minimum amount of time; they are pleasant to do; and they bring excellent results.

By means of such thinking you also change your environment. You have a better opinion of people. You more clearly see the good in them (much of which may have been hidden). This is something you can easily prove for yourself and, incidentally, it is something you ought to prove every day. When you think well of people and especially when you express that approval, you immediately set a standard for them to which they try to measure up. It is the quickest way to bring out the desired good qualities in any person.

But "environment" consists of things as well as people, and your appreciation and approval of all that is good, even in things, will sustain an awareness of their desirable qualities in your consciousness, thus making you happier. In addition, it will almost surely bring to mind something you can do to enhance the appearance, condition or usefulness of those same things, thus further increasing their desirability. Thought does change environment!

MENTAL REALIZATION

Affirmative thinking makes it possible for you to work out your plans. This is so important that you can never afford to let negation interfere. Your thought must contain the best, because you want to bring your good to fruition in the best possible way. When you are free from the negation of emotional conflict, your mind becomes a clear, pure channel through which God-Wisdom flows, and the good you desire is created for you. That is what is needed for you to be successful.

Then, too, the ability to think without the interference of negative feelings is necessary to unfold that deeper, spiritual realization which is your highest aspiration. Such realization is an unfoldment eminently deeper than intellectual accomplishment. It is such a conscious unifying of self with the Father that you are aware of a complete oneness. This is an experience you may not be able to put into words, but it is nevertheless so real that no one who experiences it can ever dispute it. It is what all humankind has forever sought, because it is the inherent nature of all people eventually to find their true relationship to God—as children of God.

Thus, clear thinking, health, happiness, friendships and prosperity are all important and worthy, but they are also steps on the stairway which we climb in our ascent to spiritual realization.

If we look at it another way, we can say that spiritual realization is the *basis* of all these expectations. In attaining a high spiritual consciousness (which we call realization) humankind is automatically assured of all these other things. It is a rule that works both ways.

HOW TO DO IT

How shall all of this be brought about? That is the practical question you want answered.

From the first page of this book—through study on the mental level—you have been learning the answer to that query. In a most simple way, you learned how your mind is constituted; how it is an expression and activity of the Mind of God; how you can use the creative power of your mind, applying it to your daily experiences. Step by step you have had a steady growth of understanding, and learned how to put that understanding to work.

One idea thoroughly understood and put into practice is vastly more valuable than reading books if nothing is done about the information thus acquired. Wide reading in a new field is, in fact, often very confusing. Therefore, get yourself so completely saturated with just a few basic principles that they are firmly established in your mind and built into your thinking as habit. You will then be ready for additional material.

THE VALUE OF PRAYER

Prayer is another part of the procedure for attaining realization. Because of the rich heritage of associations and experiences surrounding the word "prayer," it is one of the most powerful and beautiful words in our language. There is something of a benediction in just the word itself. And still, too often, it is not rightly understood. If you think of prayer as simply asking God for what you want, pleading for comfort, for supplies and coaxing God for favors, you sadly limit the meaning of this wondrous word.

Prayer is the contact of our mind with God-Mind in a way that results in bringing to physical reality a desired good. It lifts a person into an awareness of his or her relationship to the spiritual Father. That relationship implies all the rights of sonship; sonship involves the right to use and enjoy the Father's abundant supplies; and these supplies are material, emotional and spiritual.

We know that the Father is the All-surrounding Spirit,

which is everything. We know each person is entitled to his or her own rich share of that abundance. We have found that effective prayer involves the cleansing of thought, clear affirmation and right action; time spent in quietly knowing your right as a child of the One Father, realizing your privileges of sonship, and the giving of grateful thanks—all this is prayer.

No modern wording can improve upon the definition in Montgomery's fine old hymn which begins:

Prayer is the soul's sincere desire,
Uttered or unexpressed;
The motion of a hidden fire
That trembles in the breast.

For another and much older expression of it, we read in Job:

Thou shalt make thy prayer unto him, and he shall hear thee, and thou shalt pay thy vows. Thou shalt also decree a thing, and it shall be established unto thee: and the light shall shine upon thy ways.

In the very heart of this statement we find perfect assurance. There is calm, complete trust! There is perfect knowing!

ACCORDING TO YOUR FAITH

Are prayers answered? Yes, if they truly are prayers. To what degree do the answers correspond to the desired results? Jesus answers that again and again: "According to thy faith be it unto thee."

How shall we pray? Again Jesus gives explicit directions:

Enter into thy closet, and when thou has shut thy door, pray to thy Father which is in secret; and thy Father, which seeth in secret, shall reward thee openly.

What is meant by the word "closet"? A quiet room provides privacy which often encourages effective prayer.

Free from all distraction, we may enter into free and unconstrained communication with God. *Closet*, however, means much more than a private room; it means temporarily shutting the mind to everything that might interfere with the act of prayer. It means shutting the door on all worries, anxieties, fears and tensions–everything which might intrude and disrupt the direction of your thought.

You are keeping an appointment with God, securing instructions from your Father. You must not let anything interfere with that appointment. You have entered into the closet of your mind, and you are alone with God. Your prayer is a personal experience, and "the Father which seeth in secret shall reward thee openly." Afterward you go about your day's activities free from all anxiety because the Father's Wisdom is functioning in and through you. From such communion you have found new strength, happiness and guidance. The prayer-time experience has provided a sense of vitality and security. Your work can now progress only in the right way. Your affairs shall prosper. *Realization* is yours.

More than this, however, you need to remember that this joy, satisfaction and sense of oneness must translate into action in your relations with others. The rich inner experience has to be carried over into an outer expression which gives joy, courage, help or specific good of some kind to other people. To retain the value of this inner spiritual experience you must share it, express it in action. This is a necessity.

Study, prayer and realization are spiritual aspects of your endeavor; but your physical, emotional and intellectual activities also have their share in bringing about your desired good–which, in this case, is the unfoldment of your inner spiritual nature.

QUESTIONS FOR SELF-STUDY AND GREATER FOCUS

1. What particular words and ideas have you been using to create better mental habits? What success are you having?

2. Make a special effort this week to bring about more harmonious conditions in your environment. Note the results and write them here in a few words.

QUESTIONS FOR SELF-STUDY AND GREATER FOCUS

3. Find two or three Bible statements about prayer which you think are particularly helpful, and write them here.

4. How do you explain your right to claim any specific good result when you pray?

**Better Living—
Now!**

For practical purposes you want to wisely use your creative ability for physical well-being. If you are ill or in any way below what you consider par, that fact in itself is ample evidence that something needs to be done. No one wants to be ill! This is when you should assert your dominion; you should use your authority, declaring and affirming in prayer that bodily conditions now return to normal. It can be done, and knowledge that it can constitutes one of the great advancements in the modern mental-psychological-spiritual field.

The Science of Mind teaches that because you are a part of the Infinite Oneness, you can declare your perfect physical condition and it will manifest. This is definite use of spiritual Law. Your *thought*, backed by faith and conviction, is the start of your experience of physical wholeness, which becomes manifest to the extent of your belief in it.

The fact and experience of illness is not denied, but you learn to see it for what it really is—the outpicturing of a belief, idea or pattern of thought. It is but an effect, the result of a cause. It can be changed or discarded, and in its place you may establish as cause, in the creative realm of Law, the opposite creative idea—that of perfect health. Whatever is firmly planted in your mind, in absolute belief, is acted upon by the Law of Mind and *has to come forth in your world of experience.*

PHYSICAL HEALING

If bodily illness confronts you, do this at least twice a day: Get as comfortable as you can, releasing all tension. Resolve that for at least a few minutes you will forget the bodily discomfort, the pain, the fever or any other symptom which distresses you. Try to let go, to relax all over, so that all tenseness disappears from your body. Close your eyes and know that your body is the house in which God dwells, that God is in you as you, that God is what you are. Then quietly, very slowly, with ample time for a deep realization of every word, say:

There is One Life, that Life is God, that Life is perfect, that Life is my life now. My body is a manifestation of the living Spirit. It is created and sustained by the One Presence and the One Power. That Power is flowing in and through me now, animating every organ, every action and every function of my physical being. There is perfect circulation, perfect assimilation and perfect elimination. There is no congestion, no confusion and no inaction. I am One with the infinite rhythm of Life which flows through me in love, in harmony and in peace. There is no fear, no doubt and no uncertainty in my mind. I am letting that Life which is perfect flow through me. It is my life now. There is One Life; that Life is God, that Life is perfect, that Life is my life now.

You will notice that no particular discomfort was named. You have not asked for anything. You have been trying to *realize* what you *are*. This or a similar meditation should be used often during any period of illness. The big job you have is to convince yourself of your natural perfection. When all negation is wiped out of your consciousness and you feel you are a specific part of the Infinite, a child of the One Father, with God's qualities, you have then planted the idea of health in your mind and it will come forth in your body. This is what effective meditation or prayer does.

To bring healing to pass is, indeed, exercising your rightful dominion over your health.

FINANCES

To have direction over your financial affairs is of great importance and value. All that has to be done is to examine once again the basic principle. It covers all your needs. The requirement is that you understand and use the Law of infinite Mind. Whatever you believingly declare into Mind and act accordingly on, manifests in your affairs. Are you in need of money right now? Then let your meditation follow along these lines:

First of all, "enter into the closet" of your mind, the quiet, private place of your consciousness. Forget about your needs. Make yourself comfortable. Know that you are going to talk things over with your Senior Partner. You can trust God, so let your mind be at peace. Lay aside your worries. Spend a few minutes thinking about the many blessings you already have—just the simple things of life. Name some of

them and give thanks for them. Be *truly* grateful for them and
say so! Remain in perfect quietness and, speaking your
words softly, trustfully and happily, use such expressions as
these:

*Father-Mother God, I am looking to You, as Senior Partner in my busi-
ness affairs, for the guidance I need. I know I am led to see and do what
is right, so l am supplied with money for my every good need.*

*I now declare that right contacts are established, right influences are set
into motion and right activities are started so that my abundance
becomes manifest. I declare there is right action in regard to all my
affairs.*

*I know that the Universe responds to my believing word and that right
results and rewards are mine. I am guided so that I see the right people,
say and do the right things, give the right kind of service, and make
myself valuable to others. Money to meet my every good requirement is
now mine.*

*I live wholesomely and efficiently, and give generously. I know that
abundant funds for doing so are now mine, and they come to me in
exactly the right way.*

*I am grateful for this abundant supply; I give sincere thanks for it. I
have decreed it, and it is established unto me. I use it freely in the service of God and humankind, knowing that as it goes out in every way
and in loving helpfulness to others, it is constantly being blessed, and
that further money will take its place as fast as needed.*

*Now I go out and "act accordingly." I express the attitude of abundance;
I feel and look prosperous. I believe in my prosperity. And so I prosper.*

EMPLOYMENT

If this meditation is used for the purpose of finding employment, think of God as the great Business Manager who knows just where to send you for right contacts. If it is used for the improvement of your present business, take ample time to assert that new activity is now being manifest; that you are finding new ways to make your business more productive and, especially, that methods and ways of greater service come to your mind so the business will be more valuable to others. The Senior Partner in your business life can always supply you with the right plans, if you believingly decree and accept that it shall be so.

Your increased prosperity will probably involve a number of other people—their thinking, influence, cooperation and perhaps actual activity. But you do not need to know who or where they are. Your Senior Partner will look after that for you. You have dominion over your business affairs just to the degree you believe you have, and you need to act accordingly.

A NEW IDEA

Sometimes a situation arises wherein you need an entirely new idea, and you have no way of knowing what it ought to be. In that case there is no specific *thing* to claim, only an *idea*; but claiming an idea, even when you do not know what it ought to be, is just as specific as though you were claiming quick shipment of goods, a job, money to buy a house or anything else.

If this vague something—an unknown idea—is such that it would solve your difficulties, accept it. Then the central part of your creative prayer-time might be worded something like this:

Father-Mother God, as my Business Guide and Counselor, You are supplying me with exactly the right idea so I can meet all requirements. I am grateful that even when I do not know the specific idea I need, Your All-Wise Mind does know.

I shall not permit myself to be worried or hurried about any new plan. I now accept the idea I need and the wisdom to handle all the details intelligently and successfully. The right idea becomes known to me. I accept it at this moment.

At the right time it is presented to me and I shall recognize it. But, right now, this instant, I know that it is already mine. I accept it thankfully and know I have the ability to carry it out faithfully, happily and enthusiastically, knowing that it shall succeed richly.

I do my part as a worthy Junior Partner in making life a success.

This experience of accepting an idea when you have no information whatsoever as to what it ought to be, is one of the most satisfying you can ever have: Assure yourself over and over that your prayer is fulfilled. Don't worry if many days go by without there seeming to be any response. You may be sure that the right developments are taking place. Your affairs are rightly being attended to. Steps are in progress to bring your new idea to you, together with the necessary knowledge and plans for its complete fulfillment. Be still and wait. Believe. Accept.

THE DETAILS WILL COME

Then some day, all of a sudden, perhaps when your mind is busy with something entirely different, even some trivial little matter, a flash of inspiration will come and *you will know* the idea has come!

At first you may see no possible way it could be carried

out. That does not matter in the least. When God supplies an idea He is wise enough to furnish the plan for implementing it. Give happy, sincere thanks for the idea; accept it; know it is the right one. Don't listen to the objections that immediately come to mind. (They may be good sensible ones, too, insofar as you know, but they can't compare with God-Wisdom.) So when an idea comes from God through your intuition, don't be so foolish as to let old concepts interfere with it. Without any anxiety or sense of haste, mentally accept—in perfect confidence—the details of the plan by which your idea can be carried out. *They will come!*

You must, of course, go about every activity which would support your idea . . . and don't push things. God's time is the right time. Everything will be made plain for you; your Partnership will continue to be a success. The Father furnishes the ideas, plans, inspiration and courage as you are receptive to them. You, the child, carry out those plans by doing the work. The idea is the Father's. Your responsibility is to go about your work happily and successfully.

You *can* have dominion over your business affairs.

SPIRITUAL DOMINION

What is spiritual dominion? Is it not already included in these simple everyday experiences and activities? Yes and no. *Everything is Spirit.* We need always to keep that in mind. The results we have discussed are Spirit made manifest in the tangible affairs of life through spiritual Law.

Complete spiritual dominion, however, implies something more difficult to explain because it is an inner, personal experience. It is a state of awareness that you achieve as you completely accept in yourself the Father's Nature, and know that you, too, are a part of Spirit, and therefore at one with the

Father. Then you can say, as did Jesus, "I and the Father are one."

When you have a deep inner feeling that nothing separates you from God, you sense a great flood of satisfaction, peace, strength and freedom which could never come except to someone who had *chosen* to advance into a greater spiritual awareness. Remember that to go beyond the peak of your present growth demands that you *choose* to do so.

Little by little as you advance, you come into a greater experience of spiritual awareness, which is your natural right. Then you grow into ever greater spiritual dominion. Spiritual growth is the essence and beautiful action of Life Itself. This is eminently important and is the ultimate reward which reflects in your abilities and activities of daily living.

In conclusion, remember that as you grow in knowledge of God, in spiritual awareness—which is every person's goal— you come to an intelligent understanding of spiritual Law and how to use It. And through the creative action of your thought as prayer, you may realize and experience your every good desire.

And God said . . . Let them have dominion. . . .

QUESTIONS FOR SELF-STUDY AND GREATER FOCUS

1. Suppose you had a friend who was ill and wanted your help. Write a meditation of not over thirty words which you would use for his or her healing.

2. Consider that you might be out of work or wanting to build a larger business, or that you want better working conditions where you are, or you specifically want some new idea which you can develop into a worthy project.

   Choose one of these desires and write a twenty-word statement to be used as a meditation.

II

A Sensible Viewpoint
for Today's World

A deeper look at the life-changing power you have.
Some key Science of Mind perspectives.

A Deeper Look

The Science of Mind is not a personal opinion, nor is it a special revelation. It is a result of the best thought of the ages. It borrows much of its light from others but, in so doing, robs no one, for Truth is universal.

The Christian Bible, perhaps the greatest book ever written, truly points a way to eternal values. But there are many other bibles, all of which taken together weave the story of spiritual Truth into a unified pattern.

All races have had their bibles as all have had their religions; all have pointed a way to ultimate values, but can we say that any of them has really pointed **The Way**? It is unreasonable to suppose that any one person or race encompasses all truth, and alone can reveal the way of life to others.

Taking the best from all sources, the Science of Mind has

access to the highest enlightenment of the ages. **The Science of Mind reads everyman's bible and gleans the truths therein contained.** It studies all people's thought and draws from each that which is true. Without criticism, without judgment, but by true discrimination, that which is true and provable may be discovered and put to practical use.

THE SEARCH FOR TRUTH

What is the Truth? Where may it be found? And how used? These are the questions that an intelligent person asks. He or she finds the answer in the study of the Science of Mind. Shorn of dogmatism, freed from superstition and always ready for greater illumination, the Science of Mind offers the student of life the best that the world has so far discovered.

It has been well said that "religions are many; but Religion is one." The varying faiths of humankind are unnumbered, but the primal faith of the race is today, as of old, the One Faith; an instinctive reliance upon the Unseen, which we have learned to call God.

Religion is One. Faith is One. Truth is One. There is One Reality at the heart of all religions, whether their name be Hindu, Mohammedan, Christian or Jewish. Each of these faiths, limited by its outlook upon life and the universe, evolved its own specific statements of faith, called creeds and beliefs, and henceforth was governed by them.

SPIRITUAL EXPERIENCE

Spiritual experience is always a new thing; it ever seeks to express itself in a new way. The history of religion is a history of a periodic breaking away from the older body and the formulation of a new body of disciples to whom had come new light and a more satisfying experience.

While the Universal Mind contains all knowledge and is the potential of all things, only as much truth comes to us as we are able to receive. Should all the wisdom of the universe be poured over us, we should yet receive only that which we are ready to understand. Each one draws from the source of all knowledge that to which he or she inwardly listens. The scientist discovers the principle of science, the artist taps the essence of beauty, the saint draws Christ into his or her being, because to each of us is given according to our ability to receive.

Emerson taught of the immanence of God; of the spiritual impulse underlying all life; of the divinity of the universe, including mankind; and his message gradually permeated the sodden mass of the accepted theological concepts of the day. He wrought a revolution in religious thinking, the full effects of which we are only beginning to realize in our own time.

"Yourself," he said, "a new born bard of the Holy Ghost, cast behind you all conformity, and acquaint men at first hand with Deity. Look to it first and only that tradition, custom, Authority, are not bandages over your eyes, so that you cannot see. . . . Let me admonish you first of all to go alone, to refuse good models, even those sacred in the imagination of men; dare to love God without mediator and without veil." "O my brothers, God exists: There is a soul at the center of Nature, and over the will of every man, so that none of us can wrong the universe. . . . things do not happen, they are pushed from behind."

THE IMMANENCE OF GOD

The central principle of the teaching of the Science of Mind is this immanence of God. "God is an eternal and everlasting essence." All phenomena appearing in the natural world are manifestations of the spiritual world, the world of causes. "Our thought is an instrument of Divine Mind." "Christ is the reality of every man, his true inner self. Christ is the unseen principle in Man. God is in Man." The whole universe is the manifestation of a Unity which we call God.

The Science of Mind believes sincerely in what is known as "the silence," that is, it accepts the teachings of Jesus that "the Kingdom of God is within." The new sayings of Jesus from "Oxyrhyncus" quote the statement as follows: "The Kingdom of Heaven is within you and whoever knows himself shall find it. Strive therefore to know yourselves, and ye shall be aware that ye are the Sons of the almighty Father, and ye shall know that ye are in the City of God, and ye are the City."

Believing that the Universal Spirit comes to fullest consciousness in man, as his innermost Self, we strive to cultivate the inner life, knowing that religious certainty is the result of an impact of God upon the soul. We seek the witness of the Inner Spirit. We call this becoming Christ-conscious or God-conscious, meaning by that, attaining Soul-certainty.

A PRACTICAL MESSAGE

In its practice and teachings, the Science of Mind endeavors to include the whole life. It is not a dreamy, mystical cult, but the exponent of a vigorous gospel, applicable to the everyday needs of our common life. Indeed, this is the one distinctive tenet of its teaching that accounts for its rapid growth. Men and women find in it a message that fits in with their daily needs.

The conventional idea of the future life, with its teachings of rewards and punishment, is not stressed; the gospel is the good news for the here and now. Religion, it says, if it means anything, means right living, and right living and right thinking wait upon no future, but bestow their rewards in this life—in better health, happier homes and all that makes for a well-balanced, normal life.

The following is a brief statement of principles which the Science of Mind regards as true.

The Universe is fundamentally good.

Humankind is a manifestation of Spirit, and for It to desire evil for us would be for It to desire evil for Itself. This is unthinkable and impossible, for it would cause Spirit to be self-destructive; therefore, we may be certain that the Spirit of Life is for, and not against, humankind.

All apparent evil is the result of ignorance, and will disappear to the degree that it is no longer thought about, believed in or indulged in. Evil is not a thing in itself. It has no separate, independent existence and no real law to support it.

God is Love, and Love can have no desire other than to bless all alike, and to express Itself through all.

Many who had lost faith in God have, in this new manner of thinking, found what their souls had sought. The emphasis is insistently on God, ever present, ever available; and on our ability to make ourselves receptive to the inflow of the Divine Spirit. In essence, this was the primal message of the enlightened prophets of all the ages, and this is the message of the Science of Mind.

SCIENCE AND RELIGION

The thought of the ages has looked to the day when science and religion shall walk hand in hand through the visible to the invisible. A movement which endeavors to unify the great conclusions of human experience must be kept free from petty ideas, from personal ambitions, and from any attempt to promote one person's opinion. Science knows nothing of opinion but recognizes a government of law whose principles are universal. These laws, when complied with, respond alike to all. Religion becomes dogmatic and often superstitious when based on the lengthened shadow of any one personality. Philosophy intrigues us only to the extent that it sounds a universal note.

The ethics of Buddha, the morals of Confucius, the beatitudes of Jesus, together with the spiritual experiences of other great minds, constitute viewpoints of life which must not be overlooked. The mystical concepts of the ancient sage of China keep faith with the sayings of Emerson, and wherever deep cries unto deep, deep answers deep.

WHAT ALL PEOPLE SEEK

All people seek some relationship to the Universal Mind, the Over-Soul or the Eternal Spirit which we call God. Most of the deepest thinkers of the ages have concluded that we live in a spiritual universe which includes the material or physical universe. That this spiritual universe must be one of pure intelligence and perfect life, dominated by love, by reason and by the power to create, is an inevitable conclusion.

Science, philosophy, intuition and revelation all must unite in an impersonal effort if Truth is to be gained and held. Ultimately that which is true will be accepted by all. The Science of Mind endeavors to coordinate the findings of science, religion and philosophy, to find a common ground upon which true philosophic conclusions, spiritual intuitions and mystic revelations may agree with the cold facts of science, thus producing fundamental conclusions, the denial of which is not conceivable to a rational mind.

It goes without saying that such conclusions cannot contradict each other. No system of thought can stand which denies human experiences; no religion can remain vital which separates humanity from Divinity; nor can any science which denies the spontaneous appearance of volition and will in the universe maintain its position.

THE DISCOVERY OF RELIGION

Old forms and old creeds are passing, but the eternal realities abide. Religion has not been destroyed; it is being discovered. God, the great innovator, is in His world and that means that progress is by divine authority. Through all the ages, one increasing purpose runs, and that purpose can be no less than the evolution of the highest spiritual attributes of humankind. It is only the unessential that is vanishing, that the abiding may be made more clearly manifest.

Religious faith in our day is breaking from the narrow bounds of past teaching and expanding both in breadth and depth. It is not because people believe less in God and the true essentials of spiritual life, but because they must believe more; they are literally forced by the inevitable logic of facts to build for themselves concepts of the Infinite commensurate with the greatness and glory of the world in which they live.

As Emerson so truly said, "When the half-gods go the great God arrives." The Science of Mind is reaching out to a truer concept of God, immanent in the universe as the very substance, law and life of all that is. The difference between the older way of thinking and the new is that we have come to see that the One Supreme Cause and Source of all that exists, is not a separate Being outside His world, but is in fact the actual Spirit of Life shining through all creation as its very Life Principle, infinite in Its working and eternal in Its essence. The universe is none other than the Living God made manifest, so that Paul voiced a literal truth when he said: "In him we live, and move, and have our being." Such is the reverent conclusion of the Science of Mind, a faith that is winning its way in this, our new day.

A REVOLUTIONARY NEW VIEW

The religious implications of this new viewpoint of life are revolutionary. It means that there is a moral and spiritual order in the cosmos to which mankind is intimately related. Faith in God is not, as many would have us believe, a retreat from reality, a projecting of the personal wish into a cosmic postulate. Faith in God is a reasonable expanding of the facts of life to their wisest and inevitable vision and logical end; it is the logical complement of a world order, every fibre of which has a teleological meaning. Religious faith, in fact, is rooted in the facts and realities of the natural order, wrought into the very texture of life. Since supreme wisdom and life are in reality all that exist (which includes humankind), religious faith is but deep calling unto deep; God recognizing His own existence and presence.

THE END OF FEAR

The future religion will be free from fear, superstition and doubt, and will ask no one where God may be found. For the "secret place of the most High" will be revealed in the inner sanctuary of our own hearts, and the eternal God will sit enthroned in our own minds. We can know no God external to that power of perception by which alone we are conscious of anything. God must be interpreted to us *through* our own nature.

Who would know God, must be *as* God, for He who inhabits eternity also finds a dwelling place in His own creation. Standing before the altar of life in the temple of faith, we learn that we are integral parts of the universe and that it would not be complete without us. That native faith within, which we call intuition, is the direct impartation of Divine Wisdom through us. Who can doubt its gentle urges or misunderstand its meaning?

This inner life may be developed through meditation and prayer. Meditation is quiet, contemplative thought, with a definite purpose always in mind. Prayer is a receptive mental and spiritual attitude, through which a person expects to receive inspiration.

There is a Presence pervading all. There is an Intelligence running through all. There is a Power sustaining all, binding all into one perfect whole. The realization of this Presence, Intelligence, Power and Unity constitutes the nature of the mystic Christ, the indwelling Spirit, the image of God, the Sonship of the Father.

Christ means the universal idea of Sonship; the entire creation, both visible and invisible. There is One Father of all. This One Father, conceiving within Himself, gives birth to all the Divine Ideas. The sum total of all these ideas constitutes the mystic Christ.

WHO WAS JESUS?

Jesus was a man, a human being, who understood his own nature. He knew that as the human embodies the Divine, it manifests the Christ nature. Jesus never thought of himself as different from others; his whole teaching was that what he did others could do. His divine nature was aroused; he had plunged beneath the material surface of creation and found its spiritual cause. This cause, he called God or the Father. To this indwelling God, he constantly turned for help, daily guidance and counsel. To Jesus, God was an indwelling Reality, the Infinite Person in every personality. It was by the power of this Spirit that Jesus lived. He clearly understood the unity of God and person.

Every man is a potential Christ. From the least to the greatest the same life runs through all, threading itself into the patterns of our individuality. God is "over all, in all and through all." As Jesus, the man, gave way to the Divine Idea, the human took on the Christ Spirit and became the voice of God to humanity.

Conscious of his divinity, yet humble as he contemplated the infinite life around him, Jesus spoke from the height of spiritual perception, proclaiming the deathless reality of the individual life, the continuity of the individual soul, the unity of the Universal Spirit with all people.

The Science of Mind, following the example of Jesus, teaches that every person may aspire to divinity, since we are incarnations of God. It also teaches a direct relationship between God and humankind. The indwelling Spirit is God. It could be nothing less, since we have Spirit plus nothing, out of which all things are made. Behind each is the Infinite; within each is the Christ. No boundary line separates the human mind from the Mind which is God.

The Science of Mind teaches that human personality should be, and may become, the highest manifestation of God. There is a reservoir of life and power as we approach the center; it is loosed and it flows through us to the circumference as we realize the unity of the whole and our relationship to it. God is incarnated in all people and individualized through all creation without loss to Himself.

YOU ARE UNIQUE

To be an individual means to exist as an entity. As God, rightly understood, is the Infinite Person, so the Spirit is the Infinite Essence of all individuality. Within the One Supreme Mind, since It is infinite, exists the possibility of projecting limitless expressions of Itself; but since the Infinite is infinite, each expression of Itself is unique and different from any other expression. Thus the Infinite is not divided, but multiplied.

While all people have the same origin, no two are alike except in ultimate essence—"One God and Father of us all," but numberless sonships, each sonship a unique institution in the universe of wholeness. **We are all individualized centers of God-consciousness and spiritual power, as complete as we know ourselves to be, and we know ourselves only as we comprehend our relationship to the whole.**

This Presence, this inner sense of a greater Reality, bears witness to Itself through our highest acts and in our deepest emotions. Who is there who has not at times felt this inner Presence? It is impossible to escape our true nature. The voice of Truth is insistent. The urge to unfold is constant. In the long run each of us will fully express our divinity, for "good will come at last alike to all."

We stand in the shadow of a mighty Presence, while love

forever points the way to heaven. Mingled with the voice of humanity is the word of God, for Truth is a synonym for God, and whoever speaks any truth speaks the word of God. Science reveals eternal principles; mathematics, immutable laws; and illumined minds reveal the Eternal Spirit. Behind all is a unity, through all is a diversity, saturating all is a divinity.

We can no more do without religion than we can do without food, shelter or clothing. According to our belief about God will be our estimate of life here and hereafter. To believe in a God of vengeance is one thing, and to believe in a God of love and a just law of cause and effect is another.

OUR CONNECTION IS DIRECT!

To believe in a special dispensation of Providence robs us of our own immediate accessibility to goodness and creates the necessity of mediums other than our own souls, through which we must gain entrance to Reality. We cannot reach beyond the vision of our own souls. We must have direct access to the Truth.

To believe in a specialized Providence is both scientific and sensible. We are always specializing some law of nature; this is the manner in which all science advances. Unless we can thus specialize the great Law of Life Itself—the Law of Mind and Spirit—we have no possibility of further advancement in the scale of being.

The unique power that Jesus expressed resulted from his conscious union with the creative Principle which is God. Jesus realized that we are living in a spiritual universe now, and like Buddha, Plato, Socrates, Swedenborg, Emerson and Whitman, he clearly understood and taught a law of parallels or spiritual correspondences. The parables of Jesus were mostly illustrations of the concept that the laws of nature and the laws of thought are identical. This has been one of the highest perceptions of the enlightened of all ages.

A SPIRITUAL SYSTEM

The universe in which we live is a spiritual system governed by laws of Mind. There are not two minds; there is but One Mind, which is God. The out-push of the Mind of God through the human mind is the self-realization of Spirit seeking a new outlet for Its own expression. Ideas come from the Great Mind and operate through the human mind. The two are one. In this way the Infinite Mind is personal to each individual.

From the infinite self-knowingness of God, our power to know arises, because our mind springs from the Universal Mind. In this way the Infinite multiplies Itself through the finite.

The Science of Mind teaches that God is personal, and personal in a unique sense, to everyone. It teaches that conscious communion with the indwelling Spirit opens the avenues of intuition and provides a new starting point for the creative power of the Almighty.

No one ever lived who valued the individual life more than Jesus. He proclaimed his divinity through his humanity, and taught that all people are brothers and sisters. Every person comes from the bosom of the unseen Father. As the divinity of Christ is awakened through the humanity of humankind, the divine spark which is shot from the central fires of the Universal Flame warms other souls in the glow of its own self-realization.

We can give only what we have. The only shadow that we cast is the shadow of the self. This shadow lengthens as we realize the great Presence in which we live, move and have our being.

The Science of Mind not only emphasizes this unity of God and humankind, it teaches us that in such degree as our thought becomes spiritualized, it actually manifests the Power of God. In doing this, it literally follows the teaching of Jesus when he proclaimed that all things are possible to the person who believes.

WHAT IS PRAYER?

It is written that "the prayer of faith shall save the sick, and the Lord shall raise him up." It is self-evident that the prayer of faith is a positive acceptance of the good we desire. Faith is a movement within the mind. It is a certain way of thinking. It is an affirmative mental attitude. Throughout the ages the prayer of faith has been practiced by every religion and wonderful results have been obtained. There is a law governing this possibility, or else it never could have been. It is the business of the Science of Mind to view these facts, estimate their cause, and in so doing, to provide a definite knowledge of the law governing the facts.

The Science of Mind teaches that right thinking can demonstrate success and abundance; can offer help to those who are in physical distress, and bring peace to those who are lost in the maze of confusion, doubt and fear.

The Science of Mind teaches that the Kingdom of God is at hand; that there is a perfection at the center of all things, and that true salvation comes only through true enlightenment, through a more conscious and a more complete union of our lives with the Invisible.

The Science of Mind does not place undue importance either on mental healing or the law of abundance. Its main emphasis is placed not on visible things but on the Invisible. It teaches that an invisible law governs everyone's life. This law is a law of faith or belief; it is a law of mind and consciousness. This will greatly appeal to the practical person, for when the Law of our being is understood, it may be consciously used, thus providing every individual with a certain way to freedom, to happiness and to success.

The Science of Mind teaches joy; it teaches freedom from fear and uncertainty; it teaches faith, a faith justified by results. All people instinctively have faith and we all have an intuition within us which, should we follow it, would lead us inevitably to a place not only of an inner sense of certainty, but to a place of the outer condition of security.

The Divine Spirit is not limited nor does It wish to limit us. Its whole intent is to give us a more abundant life. The time has come when religion must be practical, and when faith in the invisible must be consciously developed, free from dogma, superstition and fear.

The Science of Mind today offers the world what the ages have been waiting for. It is the culmination of the hope, the aspiration and the faith of the enlightened of all time. The Truth it teaches is old; it has run through spiritual philosophies of the ages, but it has always been more or less handicapped by the dogmas and superstitions imposed upon it by the theology of its times.

The New Age demands that the fear and superstition surrounding religious conviction be removed, and that the Truth—plain, simple and direct—be presented so that all may learn to live now, in the present, with the assurance that the "eternal God is thy refuge. . . ."

III

A Summary of Important Science of Mind Principles

Ideas about life and God essential to modern spiritual understanding.
Supportive quotations from the world's timeless writings.

READER/CUSTOMER CARE SURVEY

We care about your opinions! Please take a moment to fill out our online Reader Survey at **http://survey.hcibooks.com**.
As a **"THANK YOU"** you will receive a **VALUABLE INSTANT COUPON** towards future book purchases as well as a **SPECIAL GIFT** available only online! Or, you may mail this card back to us and we will send you a copy of our exciting catalog with your valuable coupon inside.
(PLEASE PRINT IN ALL CAPS)

First Name _____ MI. _____ Last Name _____

Address _____ City _____

State _____ Zip _____ Email _____

1. Gender
- ❏ Female ❏ Male

2. Age
- ❏ 8 or younger
- ❏ 9-12 ❏ 13-16
- ❏ 17-20 ❏ 21-30
- ❏ 31+

3. Did you receive this book as a gift?
- ❏ Yes ❏ No

4. Annual Household Income
- ❏ under $25,000
- ❏ $25,000 - $34,999
- ❏ $35,000 - $49,999
- ❏ $50,000 - $74,999
- ❏ over $75,000

5. What are the ages of the children living in your house?
- ❏ 0 - 14 ❏ 15+

6. Marital Status
- ❏ Single
- ❏ Married
- ❏ Divorced
- ❏ Widowed

7. How did you find out about the book?
(please choose one)
- ❏ Recommendation
- ❏ Store Display
- ❏ Online
- ❏ Catalog/Mailing
- ❏ Interview/Review

8. Where do you usually buy books?
(please choose one)
- ❏ Bookstore
- ❏ Online
- ❏ Book Club/Mail Order
- ❏ Price Club (Sam's Club, Costco's, etc.)
- ❏ Retail Store (Target, Wal-Mart, etc.)

9. What subject do you enjoy reading about the most?
(please choose one)
- ❏ Parenting/Family
- ❏ Relationships
- ❏ Recovery/Addictions
- ❏ Health/Nutrition
- ❏ Christianity
- ❏ Spirituality/Inspiration
- ❏ Business Self-help
- ❏ Women's Issues
- ❏ Sports

10. What attracts you most to a book?
(please choose one)
- ❏ Title
- ❏ Cover Design
- ❏ Author
- ❏ Content

TAPE IN MIDDLE; DO NOT STAPLE

BUSINESS REPLY MAIL

FIRST-CLASS MAIL PERMIT NO 45 DEERFIELD BEACH, FL

POSTAGE WILL BE PAID BY ADDRESSEE

Health Communications, Inc.
3201 SW 15th Street
Deerfield Beach FL 33442-9875

I₁II₁₁₁II₁₁I₁₁I₁I₁₁I₁₁I₁II₁II₁I₁₁I₁₁I₁I₁₁₁I₁I₁I₁I₁I

FOLD HERE

Comments

A SUMMARY OF IMPORTANT SCIENCE OF MIND PRINCIPLES

*We believe in God, the Living Spirit Almighty; one indestructible, absolute, and self-existent Cause. This One manifests Itself in and through all creation. The manifest universe is the body of God; it is the logical and necessary outcome of the infinite self-knowingness of God. * * * We believe in the incarnation of the Spirit in everyone and that all people are incarnations of the One Spirit. * * * We believe in the eternality, the immortality, and the continuity of the individual soul, forever and ever expanding. * * * We believe that the Kingdom of Heaven is within us and that we experience this Kingdom in the degree that we become conscious of it. * * * We believe the ultimate goal of life to be a complete emancipation from all discord of every nature, and that this goal is sure to be attained by all. * * * We believe in the unity of all life, and that the highest God and the innermost God is one God. * * * We believe that God is personal to all who feel this Indwelling Presence. * * * We believe in the direct revelation of Truth through the intuitive and spiritual nature of the individual, and that any person may become a revealer of Truth who lives in close contact with the Indwelling God. * * * We believe that the Universal Spirit, which is God, operates through a Universal Mind, which is the Law of God; and that we are surrounded by this Creative Mind, which receives the direct impress of*

131

our thought and acts upon it. * * * We believe in the healing of the sick through the power of this Mind. * * * We believe in the control of conditions through the power of this Mind. * * * We believe in the eternal Goodness, the eternal Loving-kindness and the eternal Givingness of Life to all. * * * We believe in our own soul, our own spirit, and our own destiny; for we understand that the life of all is God.

In the following pages, the Summary of Principles is examined, point by point. In addition, the ideas presented are compared to other inspired writings and to the scriptures of many of the world's sacred traditions.

Belief in God

We believe in God, the Living Spirit Almighty . . .

G od is defined as the Deity; the Supreme Being; the Divine Presence in the universe permeating everything; the Animating Principle in everything; as Love, and the Source of guidance and of divine protection.

God has been called by a thousand different names throughout the ages. The time has now come to cast aside any points of disagreement and to realize that we are all worshiping one and the same God.

The Sacred Books of all peoples declare that God is One; a unity from which nothing can be excluded and to which nothing can be added. God is omnipotent, omnipresent and omniscient. God is our Heavenly Father and our Spiritual Mother; the Breath of our life. God is the

Changeless Reality in which we live, move and have our being.

The **Bible** says: "I am the Lord, I change not." "Forever, O Lord, thy word is settled in heaven." "One God and Father of all, who is above all, and through all, and in you all." "Know that the Lord he is God; there is none else beside him." "I am Alpha and Omega, the beginning and the ending . . . which is, and which was, and which is to come, the Almighty." "In whom are hid all the treasures of wisdom and knowledge." "God is Spirit: and they that worship him must worship him in spirit and in truth." "All things were made by him; and without him was not anything made that was made." ". . . there is but one God, the Father, of whom are all things, and we in him." ". . . the Lord he is God in heaven above, and upon the earth beneath: there is none else." "For with thee is the fountain of life; in thy light shall we see light." "God is light, and in him is no darkness at all." "Thy righteousness is an everlasting righteousness, and thy law is the truth."

From the **Text of Taoism**: "The Tao considered as unchanging, has no name." "There is no end or beginning to the Tao." "The great Tao has no name, but It effects the growth and maintenance of all things." "The Tao does not exhaust itself in what is greatest, nor is it ever absent from what is least; and therefore it is to be found complete and diffused in all things." "Thus it is that the Tao produces [all things], nourishes them . . . nurses them, completes them, matures them, maintains them, and overspreads them."

GOD AS ONENESS

The **Hermetic Teaching** defines God as a ". . . Power that naught can e'er surpass, a Power with which no one can make comparison of any human thing at all . . ." This teaching defines God as a Oneness which is the ". . . Source and Root of all, is in all things . . ." "His being is conceiving of all things. . . . He ever makes all things, in heaven, in air, in earth, in deep, in all of cosmos [that is, in the entire universe]. . . . For there is naught in all the world that is not He." "God is united to all men as light to the sun."

From the **Sacred Books of the East**: "There is but one Brahma which is Truth's self. It is from our ignorance of that One that god-heads have been conceived to be diverse." "As the sun, manifesting all parts of space, above, between, and below, shines resplendent, so over-rules the all-glorious adorable God . . ." "The One God, who is concealed in all beings, who pervades all, who is the inner soul of all beings, the ruler of all actions, who dwells in all beings . . ." "God is permanent, eternal and therefore existence itself." "All is the effect of all, One Universal Essence." "The Supreme Soul hath another name, that is, Pure Knowledge."

The **Zend-Avesta** defines God as "Perfect Holiness, Understanding, Knowledge, The most Beneficent, The uncomparable One, The All-seeing One, The healing One, The Creator."

The **Koran** says that "He is the Living One. No God is there but He."

In **Buddhism** we find these thoughts: ". . . the Supreme Being, the Unsurpassed, the Perceiver of All Things, the Controller, the Lord of All, the Maker, the Fashioner . . . the Father of All Beings. . ."

In the **Apocrypha** we read that God is ". . . the Most High who knows . . . who nourishes all. The Creator who has planted his sweet Spirit in all . . . There is One God . . . Worship him . . . who alone exists from age to age . . ."

From the **Talmud**: "Our God is a living God." "His power fills the universe . . . He formed thee; with His Spirit thou breathes."

2   Indestructible and Absolute

We believe in God, the Living Spirit Almighty; one indestructible,
absolute and self-existent Cause.

In the Science of Mind **self-existent** is defined as "living by virtue of its own being." An absolute and self-existent Cause, then, means that Principle, that Power, and that Presence which makes everything out of Itself, which contains and sustains everything within Itself. God is absolute and self-existent Cause. Therefore, the Divine Spirit contains within Itself infinite imagination, complete volition and absolute power.

We are to think of God not as **some power**, but as **All Power**; not as **some presence**, but as **the Only Presence**; not merely as **a god**, but as **The God**. Spirit is the supreme and the only Causation.

Emerson said, "There is, at the surface, infinite variety of things; at the center there is simplicity of cause." "We are escorted on every hand through life by spiritual agents, and a beneficent purpose lies in wait for us." Emerson believed that we are all sleeping giants: "Sleep lingers all our life time about our eyes, as night hovers all day in the boughs of the fir tree." "Into every intelligence there is a door which is never closed, through which the creator passes."

It Fills
the Universe

*This One manifests Itself in and through all creation
but is not absorbed by Its creation.*

The Science of Mind regards **creation** as "the giving of form to the substance of Mind. . . . The whole action of Spirit must be within Itself upon Itself." Creation is the play of Life upon Itself; the action of a limitless Imagination upon an infinite Law.

What God thinks, He energizes. The universe is God's thought made manifest. The ideas of God take innumerable forms. The manifest universe springs from the Mind of God.

The **Bible** says that "the Lord by wisdom hath founded the earth: by understanding hath he established the heavens." "In the beginning God created the heaven and the earth." "By his spirit he hath garnished the heavens." "For he spake, and it was done; he commanded, and it stood fast." ". . . the worlds were framed by the word of God . . ." "The heavens declare the glory of God; and the firmament sheweth his handiwork."

The **Hermetic Philosophy** states that "with Reason, not with hands, did the World-maker make the universal World . . ."

From a **Hindu Scripture**: "From the unmanifest springs the manifest." "Mind, being impelled by a desire to create, performs the work of creation by giving form to Itself."

Everything that exists is a manifestation of the Divine Mind; but the Divine Mind, being inexhaustible and limitless, is never caught in any form; It is merely expressed by that form. The manifest universe, then, is the Body of God. As our Statement of Principles reads: **"It is the logical and necessary outcome of the infinite self-knowingness of God."** God's self-knowingness energizes that which is known, and that which God knows takes form. The form itself has a Divine Pattern within it.

COPIES OF THE TRUTH

In the **Hermetic Teaching** we find this remarkable statement: "All things, accordingly, that are on earth . . . are not the Truth; they're copies [only] of the True. Whenever the appearance doth receive the influx from above, it turns into a copy of the Truth; without its energizing from above, it is left false. Just as the portrait also indicates the body in the picture, but in itself is not the body, in spite of the appearance of the thing that's seen. 'Tis seen as having eyes; but it sees naught, hears naught at all.

"The picture, too, has all the other things, but they are

false, tricking the sight of the beholders—these thinking that they see what's true, while what they see is really false. All, then, who do not see what's false see truth. If, then, we thus do comprehend, or see, each one of these just as it really is, we really comprehend and see. But if [we comprehend, or see, things] contrary to that which is, we shall not comprehend, nor shall we know aught true."

One of the problems addressed by the Science of Mind is to distinguish between that which is temporal and that which is eternal. God, or Spirit, is the only Reality, the One Substance or Essence. The material universe is real as a manifestation of life, but it is an effect. This is why Jesus told us to judge not according to appearances.

The **Talmud** says that "unhappy is he who mistakes the branch for the tree, the shadow for the substance."

In **Hebrews** we find: "For Christ is not entered into the holy places made with hands, which are the figures of the true; but into heaven itself, now to appear in the presence of God for us."

And from **Colossians**: "Let no man therefore judge you in meat, or in drink, or in respect of an holyday, or of the new moon, or of the sabbath days: Which are a shadow of things to come; but the body is of Christ."

Back of all form there is a Divine Substance. Hid within every appearance there is an adequate cause. If we judge by the appearance alone, as though it were self-created, we are mistaking the shadow for the Substance.

In **Fragments of a Faith Forgotten** it says: "Gain for yourselves, ye sons of Adam, by means of these transitory things . . . that which is your own, and passeth not away."

We are to translate all creation into spiritual Causation. Then we shall be viewing it rightly. The created form has no being of itself; it is an effect. In **Ramacharaka** we read: "That which is unreal hath no shadow of Real Being, notwithstanding the illusion of appearance and false knowledge. And that which hath Real Being hath never ceased to be—*can never cease to be*, in spite of all appearances to the contrary."

A DIVINE PATTERN

There is a Divine Pattern, a spiritual prototype, in the Mind of God which gives rise to all form. Jesus saw through the form to the Pattern, for he was quickened by the Spirit. "It is the spirit that quickeneth: the flesh profiteth nothing . . ." "For [now] we know in part, and we prophesy in part. But when that which is perfect is come, then that which is in part shall be done away." "Now we see as through a glass darkly." That is, our spiritual vision is not quickened to a complete perception of the Divine Reality, the spiritual prototype back of the image.

All scriptures warn us to beware of false judgments; to judge not according to appearances but to plunge beneath or through the objective form to its spiritual cause. This does not mean that the physical universe is an illusion; it does mean that it is a logical and necessary expression of the Divine Mind. If we were to think of the physical universe as the shadow of its spiritual Reality, we should be rightly interpreting it.

The Science of Mind translates physical form into mental and spiritual causation. It does not do this by denying the form, but through a right interpretation of it. The visible is an evidence of the invisible. The invisible is the cause, the visible is the effect.

4 Spirit Incarnates in Everyone

*We believe in the incarnation of the Spirit in everyone
and that all people are incarnations of the One Spirit.*

All scriptures declare that humankind is the spiritual image and likeness of God. This is emphatically revealed in the inspiration of our own scripture which says: "God created man in his own image." "The spirit of God hath made me, and the breath of the Almighty hath given me life." "Hereby know we that we dwell in him, and he in us, because he hath given us of his Spirit." "Thou hast made him a little lower than the angels, and hast crowned him with glory and honour. Thou madest him to have dominion over the works of thy hands; thou hast put all things under his feet." "Be ye therefore perfect, even as your Father which is in heaven is perfect."

"Now there are diversities of gifts, but the same Spirit." "There is one body, and one Spirit . . . one Lord, one faith, one baptism, one God and Father of all, who is above all, and through all, and in you all." "One faith, one baptism" means that through faith and intuition we realize that we are living in one Spirit, or, as Emerson said, "There is one Mind common to all individual men."

"Have we not all one Father? Hath not one God created us?" "To us there is but one God, the Father, of whom are all things." "Beloved, now are we the sons of God." "Ye are the sons of the living God." "And because ye are sons, God has sent forth the Spirit of his son into your hearts." In other words, there is but one son of God, which includes the whole human family, and the spirit of this son, which is the Spirit of Christ, is incarnated in everyone. Therefore, the Bible says that "he [humankind] is the image and glory of God."

EACH PERSON: PART OF GOD

"Know ye not that your body is the temple of the Holy Ghost which is in you . . . therefore glorify God in your body, and in your spirit, which are God's." "That which is born of the Spirit is spirit." We could have no more definite statement of the divine Incarnation than this. Every person is an incarnation of God. Since God is the Universal Spirit, the one and only Mind, Substance, Power and Presence that exists, and since all people are individuals, it follows that each person is an individualized center of the Consciousness of the One God.

When Jesus said, "I and my Father are one," but "my Father is greater than I," he was stating a mathematical proposition. Every person is an incarnation of God, but no single incarnation of God can exhaust the Divine Nature.

Everyone can use the figure "7" to infinity without ever exhausting its possibility. The more Divine Power we use, the more Divine Power is placed at our disposal, for "there is that which scattereth, and yet increaseth."

Not only is every individual an incarnation of God, and therefore a manifestation of Christ, but since each individual is unique, every person has access to God in a personal sense. The Spirit is most certainly personal to each one of us—individually and uniquely personal. We could not ask for a more complete union than this, for the union is absolute, immediate and dynamic.

DOMINION OVER EVIL

According to the revelation of the ages, humankind has a spiritual birthright which gives us dominion over all evil. But the old person must be put off; that is, transmuted into the new person, which is Christ. The real spiritual man is here now, if we could see him. Ignorance of this fact produces all evil, all limitation, all fear. A sense of separation from our source begets all our troubles. In the midst of the possibility of freedom we are bound. Thus, the **Hermetic Philosophy** states that though we are born of harmony, we have become slaves, because we are overcome by sleep. And the **Bible** says that we must awake from this sleep; that we must arise from the dead in order that Christ may give us life.

The **Koran** says: "We created man: and we know what his soul whispereth to him, and we are closer to him than his neck-vein."

In the **Talmud** we read: "First no atom of matter, in the whole vastness of the universe, is lost; how then can man's soul, which is the whole world in one idea be lost?"

The following quotations are drawn from various **Hindu**

Scriptures: "The ego [i.e., the True Self] is beyond all disease . . . free from all imagination, and all-pervading." "As from a . . . fire, in a thousand ways, similar sparks proceed, so beloved are produced living cells of various kinds from the Indestructible." "If ye knew God as he ought to be known, ye would walk under seas, and the mountains would move at your call." (This is similar to the teaching of Jesus, when he said that if we had faith the size of a grain of mustard seed, we could say unto the mountain, "Remove hence to yonder place.") "There is that within every soul which conquers hunger, thirst, grief, delusion, old age and death."

BIG SELF AND LITTLE SELF

Perhaps one of the most remarkable sayings about the self in the **Scriptures of India** is the following: "Let him raise the self by the Self and not let the self become depressed; for verily is the Self the friend of the self, and also the Self the self's enemy; The Self is the friend of the self of him in whom the self by the Self is vanquished; but to the unsubdued self the Self verily becometh hostile as an enemy." This, of course, refers to the deathless Self, the incarnation of God in us.

"He who knows himself has come to know his Lord . . ." This refers to the complete unity of the Spirit, or, as Jesus said, "I and the Father are one." "And he who thus hath learned to know himself, hath reached that God which doth transcend abundance . . ."

From the **Text of Taoism** are gathered the following inspiring thoughts: "Man has a real existence, but it has nothing to do with place; he has continuance, but it has nothing to do with beginning or end." "He whose whole mind is thus fixed emits a Heavenly light. In him who emits this heavenly light men see the [True] man."

Referring to the one whose mind is fixed on Reality, "His sleep is untroubled by dreams; his waking is followed by no sorrows. His spirit is guileless and pure; his soul is not subject to weariness." In spiritual revelation a calm contemplation of spiritual Truth is held important. The mind must be like a mirror if it is to reflect or image forth the Divine Prototype, the incarnation of God in humankind. "Men do not look into running water as a mirror, but into still water; it is only the still water that can arrest them all, and keep them in the contemplation of their real selves."

The **Hermetic Philosophy** tells us that if we would know God we must be like Him, for "like is knowable to like alone." "Make thyself to grow to the same stature as the Greatness which transcends all measure . . ." "Conceiving nothing is impossible unto thyself, think thyself deathless and able to know all—all arts, all sciences, the way of every life." It tells us to awake from our deep sleep, as though our spiritual eyes were dulled by too much looking on effect and too little contemplation of cause.

Eternal and Immortal

*We believe in the eternality, the immortality and the
continuity of the individual soul, forever and ever expanding.*

If we are incarnations of God, then our spirit is God
individualized, and as such it must be eternal. Since it
is impossible to exhaust the limitless nature of the Divine,
our expansion must be an eternal process of unfolding from
a limitless Center.

Immortality is not something we purchase. It is not a bar-
gain we make with the Almighty. It is the gift of heaven. It is
inherent in our divine nature. When the disciples of Jesus
asked him what is God's relationship to the dead, he
answered as we should expect one to answer who had
already plunged beneath the material surface of things and

149

discovered their spiritual cause. He said, "He is not a God of the dead, but of the living: for all live unto him."

God is Life, and that which is Life cannot produce death. What we call death is but a transition from one plane or one mode of expression into another. "In my Father's house are many mansions."

Jesus said to one who passed with him, "Today shalt thou be with me in paradise." In the philosophy of this spiritual genius, this God-saturated man, death was but a transition.

The **Gita** tells us, "He is not born, nor doth he die; nor having been, ceaseth he any more to be; unborn, perpetual, eternal and ancient, he is not slain when the body is slaughtered."

From the **Bible**: "He asked life of thee, and thou gavest it him, even length of days for ever and ever." "And this is the promise that he hath promised us, even eternal life." "To an inheritance incorruptible, and undefiled, and that fadeth not away, reserved in heaven for you."

6

The Kingdom
of Heaven

*We believe that the Kingdom of Heaven is within us and that we
experience this Kingdom in the degree that we become conscious of it.*

The Kingdom of Heaven means the kingdom of harmony, of peace, of joy and of wholeness. It is an inward kingdom. This is why Jesus said that we should not lay up treasures on earth, but "lay up for yourselves treasures in heaven."

Heaven is not a place but an inward state of consciousness. It is an inward awareness of Divine Harmony and Truth. It is the "house not made with hands, eternal in the heavens." Ezekiel said, "The spirit took me up, and brought me into the inner court; and, behold, the glory of the Lord filled the house." The glory of God fills everyone's consciousness who is aware of that glory.

Jesus likened the Kingdom of Heaven to a child: "Except ye be converted, and become as little children, ye shall not enter into the kingdom of heaven." This refers to the child-like consciousness, to a simple trust in the goodness of God.

The Spirit has placed divine intuition within everyone. This divine intuition is the gateway through which the inspiration of the Almighty enters the mind. This is why the Psalms tell us to "lift up our gates." That is, lift up the intuition and permit the Divine Light to enter.

DIVINE KINGDOM ALREADY ESTABLISHED

When Jesus said that we are to be perfect even as God within us is perfect, he certainly implied that there is such a Divine Kingdom already established within us. "When the without shall become as the within" then the Kingdom of God shall be established here and now. Jesus said that we should assume a childlike attitude toward this Kingdom. "Whosoever therefore shall humble himself as this little child, the same is greatest in the kingdom of heaven." "And when he was demanded of the Pharisees, when the kingdom of God should come, he answered them and said, The kingdom of God cometh not with observation: Neither shall they say, Lo here! or, lo there! for, behold, the kingdom of God is within you." This certainly refers to a state of inner awareness.

The kingdom to which Jesus referred is not external but within. It is not to be placed outside the self, neither "Lo here! or, lo there!" but it is to be perceived as an everlasting dominion within. The Kingdom of Heaven is something we possess but have not been conscious of. It is not some far-off divine event, "for the kingdom of heaven is at hand." It is neither in the mountain nor at Jerusalem, but within the mind.

Jesus likened the Kingdom of Heaven ". . . unto treasure hid in a field; the which when a man hath found, he hideth, and for joy thereof goeth and selleth all that he hath, and buyeth that field." The treasure of the inner kingdom is already hid at the center of our being and when we discover it, great joy follows. Our whole desire is to possess this inner kingdom; to drill deep into the wellspring of our being and bring up the pure oil of Spirit; to tunnel the granite rock of our unbelief and at the center of our being, discover "the pearl of great price."

THE VALUE OF PARABLES

"And the disciples came, and said unto him, Why speakest thou unto them in parables? He answered and said unto them, Because it is given unto you to know the mysteries of the kingdom of heaven, but to them it is not given." On first reading, this sounds as though Jesus were withholding his teaching from the common multitude, but such was not the case. He spoke in parables, realizing that those who comprehended their meaning would understand his teaching, for he had already instructed his disciples in the mysteries of the kingdom. That is, he had directly taught them the inner meaning of life.

In Corinthians it says: "But we speak the wisdom of God in a mystery, even the hidden wisdom, which God ordained before the world unto our glory." This is a direct reference to the inseparable unity between God and man. God has ordained that forever man shall be one with His own being, that the kingdom of good shall forever be at hand. Since we are individuals, God has also ordained that our good shall make its appearance when we recognize it.

Emerson said, "Nature forevermore screens herself from

the profane, but when the fruit is ripe it will fall." The inner mysteries of the Kingdom of God are hid from the vulgar, not because the Divine withholds Itself, but because only to the pure in heart, to the childlike in mind, can the Kingdom be revealed.

One of the greatest of the Greek philosophers said that this kingdom is something which every man possesses but which few men use. Encased in materiality, filled with the din of objective confusion, we do not hear the still small voice which evermore proclaims, "Look unto me, and be ye saved, all the ends of the earth."

A GRAIN OF MUSTARD SEED

Again, Jesus likened the Kingdom unto ". . . a grain of mustard seed, which a man took, and sowed in his field. . ." He then goes on to say that very soon this small seed becomes a tree which puts forth branches. Here Jesus is referring to the Tree of Life, which means the unity of God with man. The seed is the consciousness of the little child which becomes aware of its relationship to the Divine Parentage. Out of this inner awareness grows and blossoms a concept of harmony. The Tree of Life expands and puts forth branches; its shade provides shelter.

No matter how small our concept of heaven may be to begin with, it has the possibility of eternal unfoldment. The power to live is within the self, implanted by the Divine. Ultimately every person will realize his or her inner kingdom, which will become to that person as the Tree of Life, providing food and shelter, perfection and joy.

Again Jesus said, "The kingdom of heaven is like unto leaven, which a woman took, and hid in three measures of meal, till the whole was leavened." He is referring to the action of consciousness of the Kingdom of God in the mind as yeast spreading through the whole lump of mortal thought, lifting the weight of the burdens of life into lightness. Jesus is referring to the Kingdom of God as the Bread of Life; the eternal Substance upon which the soul feeds; the everlasting Presence upon which the inner eye feasts; the house not made with hands, in which the Spirit dwells forever.

THE PEARL OF GREAT PRICE

Again, "the kingdom of heaven is like unto a merchant man, seeking goodly pearls: Who, when he had found one pearl of great price, went and sold all that he had, and bought it." Since the greater includes the lesser, Jesus told us that we are first to seek the Kingdom because everything is included in it. "Pearl" stands for purity and perfection. When we discover the purity and perfection at the center of our own being, we shall naturally sell the dross, the fear and the doubt that infest our thought world, in order that we may possess this inner purity, that we may become conscious of this inner perfection.

Jesus did not wish us to feel that, in seeking this inner kingdom, we are losing anything worthwhile in the outer life, for he said that everyone who has sought the inner kingdom shall "receive manifold more in this present time, and in the world to come life everlasting." This is in line with all the other teachings of Jesus, that the reward for right living is immediate. The Kingdom is not something reserved only for future states; it is something which we experience here and now through the manifold blessings which the Spirit automatically bestows on us when we seek first things first.

In his parable likening the Kingdom of Heaven unto the

ns, Jesus clearly teaches that every person possesses the Oil of Spirit and that one need borrow from another.

The Kingdom of God is not something we create, not something we purchase, but something that we must realize—it is something we become inwardly aware of. There is a perfection at the center of our being. Browning tells us that we must loose this imprisoned splendor, while Plato and his followers taught that "over yonder" there is a prototype of perfection. With them "over yonder" had a meaning identical with the teaching of Jesus that the Kingdom of Heaven is within. The Greek philosophers taught that when the image, that is, the external, turns to its prototype, it is instantly made whole because it is instantly unified with its inner perfection.

THE INNER KINGDOM

Let us see what other bibles of the world have taught about this inner kingdom.

In the **Text of Taoism** we find this: "Without going outside his door . . . without looking out from his window, one sees the Tao of Heaven. The farther one goes from himself the less he knows." "What is heavenly is internal; what is human is external. If you know the operation of what is heavenly . . . you will have your root in what is heavenly . . ." "Take the days away and there will be no year; without what is internal there will be nothing external." "He who knows . . . completion . . . turns in on himself and finds there an inexhaustible store."

The **Gita** tells us: "He who is happy within him, rejoiceth within him, is illumined within, becomes eternal." And in **Fragments of a Faith Forgotten** it says: ". . . the Kingdom of Heaven is within you; and whosoever shall know himself shall find it." "Seek for the great and the little shall be added unto you. Seek for the heavenly and the earthly shall be added unto you."

In the **Upanishads** we read: "As far as mind extends, so far extends heaven." "In heaven there is no fear . . . it is without hunger or thirst and beyond all grief."

The **Pistis Sophia** says: "Be ye diligent that ye may receive the mysteries of Light and enter into the height of the Kingdom of Light."

The End of Discord

We believe the ultimate goal of life to be a complete emancipation from all discord of every nature, and that this goal is sure to be attained by all.

The ultimate goal of life does not mean that we shall ever arrive at a spiritual destination where everything remains static and inactive. What seems to our present understanding to be an ultimate goal, will, when attained, be but the starting point for a new and further evolution. We believe in an eternal upward spiral of existence. This is what Jesus meant when he said, "In my Father's house are many mansions."

The **Koran** tells us that God has made many heavens, one on top of another, which means that evolution is eternal. The **Hermetic philosophy** taught an infinite variation of the manifestation of life on an ever-ascending scale. All evolution proves the transition of the lesser into the greater.

The original sources of spiritual thought, from which the great religious conceptions of the ages have been drawn, have taught that evolution is an eternal manifestation of life on an ascending scale. As we ascend from a lower to a higher level, the limitations of the previous experience must drop away from us. Since the Kingdom of God or the Kingdom of Reality is already established in Spirit, our transition from one plane to another is a matter of consciousness, and since all persons are incarnations of the Divine Spirit, every soul will ultimately find complete emancipation, not through losing itself in God, but rather, through finding God in itself.

Tagore tells us that Nirvana is not absorption but immersion. Browning said that we are all Gods though in the germ. Jesus proclaimed that the Kingdom of Heaven is within, and that we shall attain this kingdom in such degree as we become consciously aware of and unified with it. This does not mean that there is any finality to evolution, for every apparent ultimate is but the beginning of a new experience.

8

Only
One God

*We believe in the unity of all life, and that the highest God
and the innermost God is one God.*

The enlightened in every age have taught that back of all things there is One Unseen Cause. This teaching of Unity . . . "The Lord our God is one God . . ." is the chief cornerstone of the sacred scriptures of the East, as well as our own sacred writings. It is the mainspring of the teachings of modern spiritual philosophies, such as Unity Teachings, the New Thought Movement, the Occult Teachings, the Esoteric or Inner Teachings, our own Science of Mind and even much that is taught under the name of psychology. Science has found nothing to contradict this unity, for it is self-evident.

There is One Life of which we are a part; One Intelligence, which we use; One Substance, which takes manifold forms. "That they all may be one; as thou, Father, art in me, and I in thee, that they also may be one in us."

In the **Bible** we find these passages: "Now there are diversities of gifts, but the same Spirit." "Whither shall I go from thy spirit? or whither shall I flee from thy presence? If I ascend up into heaven, thou art there: if I make my bed in hell, behold, thou art there . . . If I say, Surely the darkness shall cover me; even the night shall be light about me." "We all, with open face beholding as in a glass the glory of the Lord, are changed into the same image . . . by the Spirit of the Lord." "I shall be satisfied when I awake with thy likeness."

"Know ye not that your body is the temple of the Holy Ghost which is in you?" "That which is born of the Spirit is spirit." "The Lord our God is one God . . . He is God in heaven above and upon the earth beneath. There is none else." ". . . His word is in mine heart as a burning fire shut up in my bones." "And the Word was made flesh, and dwelt among us . . ." ". . . I will put my words in his mouth . . . the word is very nigh unto thee, in thy mouth, and in thy heart, that thou mayest do it."

THE MYSTICAL MARRIAGE

All sacred scriptures have proclaimed the unity of life; that every person is a center of God Consciousness. This is the meaning of the mystical marriage, or the union of the soul with its Source. Jesus boldly proclaimed that he was one with the Father. This is the basis for all New Thought teaching: the spiritual union of all life.

The **Qabbalah** states that "every existence tends toward the higher, the first unity . . . the whole universe is one, complex. The lower emanates from the Higher and is Its image. The Divine is active in each."

Unity is a symbol of the soul's oneness with the Higher Nature, implying complete freedom from bondage to anything less than itself. All positive religions have taught that the supreme end of humanity is a union of the soul with God.

"The Atman, which is the substratum of the ego in man, is One." The **Hermetic Teaching** tells us that "this Oneness, being source and root of all, is in all." And the Gita explains that "when he [humankind] perceiveth the diversified existence of beings as rooted in One, and spreading forth from It, then he reacheth the eternal."

Again the **Bible** tells us: "Thus saith the Lord . . . I am the first and I am the last . . ." "I am Alpha and Omega, the beginning and the ending . . . which was and which is to come . . ." "One God and Father of all, who is above all, and through all, and in you all."

From **The Awakening of Faith**: "In the essence [of Reality] there is neither anything which has to be included, nor anything which has to be added."

In one of the **Upanishads** we find this quotation: "The One God who is concealed in all beings, who is the inner soul of all beings, the ruler of all actions . . ." "All is the effect of all, One Universal Essence."

In **Echoes from Gnosis** we find: "O Primal Origin of my origination; Thou Primal Substance of my substance; Breath of my breath, the breath that is in me."

From the **Bible**: "To us there is but one God, the Father, of whom are all things, and we in him . . ." And from another bible, "All this universe has the Deity for its life. That Deity is Truth, who is the Universal Soul."

From the **Apocrypha**: "He is Lord of Heaven, sovereign of earth, the One existence." And the **Upanishads** tell us, "He who is the Ear of the ear, the Mind of the mind, the Speech of the speech, is verily the Life of life, the Eye of the eye."

A PROCESS OF AWAKENING

The Science of Mind teaches an absolute union of humankind with our Source. So complete is this union that the slightest act of human consciousness manifests some degree of our divinity. We are not God, but we have no life separate from the Divine; we have no existence apart from our Source. We think God's thoughts after Him. We are divine neither by will nor through choice, but by necessity. The whole process of evolution is a continual process of awakening. It is an understanding of this indwelling union which constitutes the Spirit of Christ.

The Science of Mind defines Christ as "the Word of God manifest in and through humankind. In a liberal sense, the Christ means the Entire Manifestation of God and is, therefore, the Second Person of the Trinity. Christ is Universal Idea, and each one 'puts on the Christ' to the degree that he or she surrenders a limited sense of Life to the Divine Realization of wholeness and unity with Good, Spirit, God."

Christ is the Higher Self, the Divine Life proceeding from the Father. This Christ enters the world of manifestation and animates all things. Christ is in everything; we are rooted and centered in Him who is "the way, the truth, and the life."

Christ is the supreme ideal which Jesus made manifest through the power of his word. Christ is the Divine Nature of all being and the Supreme Goal of Union toward which all individual and collective evolution moves.

The realization of this union gives birth to the consciousness of Christ in the individual, and has been called "the light of the world." When Peter said to Jesus, "Thou art the Christ, the son of the living God," Jesus answered by telling Peter that no man had revealed this to him but that it was a direct revelation of the Spirit.

God
Is Personal

We believe that God is personal to all who feel
this Indwelling Presence. . . . We believe in the direct revelation of Truth
through the intuitive and spiritual nature of the individual,
and that any person may become a revealer of Truth
who lives in close contact with the Indwelling God.

Know ye not that ye are the temple of God, and that the Spirit of God dwelleth in you? "God is in his holy temple." Augustine said that the pure mind is a holy temple for God, and Emerson wrote that God builds His temple in the heart. Seneca said that "temples are not to be built for God with stones . . . He is to be consecrated in the breast of each."

Every person is an incarnation of God, and since each person is an individual, everyone is a unique incarnation. We believe in the Divine Presence as Infinite Person, and personal to each. God is not *a* person, but *the* Person. This Person is an Infinite Presence filled with warmth, color and responsiveness, immediately and intimately personal to each individual.

The Spirit is both an over-dwelling and an indwelling Presence. We are immersed in It, and It flows through us as our very life. Through intuition we perceive and directly reveal God. We do not have to borrow our light from another. Nothing could be more intimate than the personal relationship between the individual and that Divine Presence which is both the Center and the Source of a person's being.

Not *some* people, but *all* people, are divine. But all people have not yet recognized their divinity. Our spiritual evolution is a gradual awakening to the realization that the Spirit is center, source and circumference of all being. It is in everything, around everything and through everything, and It is everything.

The main body of the Christian religion is built upon three grand concepts: first, that *God is an Over-dwelling Presence;* next, that *God is also an Indwelling Presence;* and third, that *the conscious union of the Indwelling and the Over-dwelling, through the human mind, gives birth to the divine child, the Christ, the Son of God.* It was this revelation which enabled Jesus to perform his wonderful works. He became so conscious of his union with God that the very words he spoke were the Words of God spoken through him.

The only way that the Power of God can be manifest through us is by our realization that the Father dwelleth in whoever doeth the works. Everyone should practice this close and intimate relationship between the individual and the Universal. Everyone should practice the Presence of

God. This Presence is a reality, the one, great and supreme reality of life. There is a "light which lighteth every man." Humankind is spoken of in the Bible as "the candle of the Lord," and Jesus said, "Let your light so shine before men, that they may see your good works, and glorify your Father which is in heaven."

Through spiritual intuition Jesus perceived his union with God. What suffering, what unuttered anguish, what persistence, effort and discipline this man may have gone through to arrive at this exalted state, we know not, but we may be gratefully aware that he passed through every gamut of human suffering and emerged triumphant, supreme. Christ is the divine and universal Emanation of the Infinite Spirit incarnated in everything, individualized in humankind and universalized in God.

UNIVERSAL . . . INDIVIDUAL

Whatever God is in the universal, humankind is in the individual. This is why all spiritual leaders have told us that if we would uncover the hidden possibility within, we should not only discover the true Self, the Christ, we should also uncover the true God, the One and only Cause, the Supreme Being, the Infinite Person.

Jesus taught a complete union of humankind with God. He proclaimed that all people are divine; that all are one with the Father; that the Kingdom of Heaven is within; that the Father has delivered all power unto the son; and that the son thinks the thoughts of God after Him, and imbibes spiritual power through realization of his union with his Source.

10 The Universal Mind

We believe that the Universal Spirit, which is God,
operates through a Universal Mind, which is the Law of God;
and that we are surrounded by this Creative Mind,
which receives the direct impress of our thought and acts upon it.

This quote explores the practical use of spiritual Power. In the Science of Mind we differentiate between Spirit, Mind and Body, just as all the great major religions have done. Spirit is the conscious and active aspect of God, as distinguished from the passive, receptive and form-taking aspect. Spirit imparts motion and manifests Itself through form. Thus, the ancients said that Spirit uses matter as a sheath.

Philo, often called Philo Judaeus, born about 10 B.C., one of the greatest of the Jewish philosophers of the Alexandrian school, said that the Active Principle, which is Spirit, is absolutely free and that the passive principle is set in motion by the Spirit, giving birth to form. Plotinus, considered the greatest of the Neo-Platonists, taught that Spirit, as Active Intelligence, operates upon an unformed substance, which is passive to It, and that through the power of the Word of Spirit this substance takes form and becomes the physical world.

The spiritual teachings of antiquity all taught a trinity or threefold unity. In order that anything may exist there must be an active principle of self-assertion, acting as law upon a passive principle, which Plotinus called an indeterminate substance, whose business it is to receive the forms which the contemplation (the word or the thought) of Spirit gives to it. In the Science of Mind, following the example of the Christian scriptures, we have named this trinity, "The Father, Son, and Holy Ghost." The Father, the supreme creative Principle; the Son (the Christ), the universal manifestation of the Father; and the supreme Law of Cause and Effect, the servant of the Spirit throughout the ages.

THE LIGHT OF THE WORLD

The Father means Absolute Being, the Unconditioned First Cause, the Source of all that is. Jesus called this Life Force "The Father." He referred to himself, and to all other people, as "The Son." "He is the image of the invisible God . . ." The ancient Hindus referred to The Son as Atman, the innermost spiritual self. Atman is the manifestation of Brahma as individuality. Each person is an individualized center of the Consciousness of God. The Christian scripture refers to the same self when it speaks of Christ in us, for the Christ Principle has a meaning identical with Atma-Buddhi, which means divine illumination, "the Light of the world."

The **Bible** says that "the first man (Adam) is of the earth
. . . the second man is the Lord from heaven." This refers
first to the physical being, formed after the manner of all creation, and next to the Christ Principle animating this being.
The birth of Christ, through Jesus, was the awakening of his
consciousness to a realization of his union with God—"I and
my Father are one."

Jesus clearly taught that all people must come to this realization if they would enter into the kingdom of harmony, into
conscious union with God, and thus gain wholeness.

From **The Perfect Way**: "The first Adam is of the earth,
earthy, and liable to death. The second is 'from heaven,' and
triumphant over death. For 'sin has no more dominion over
him.' He, therefore, is the product of a soul purified from
defilement by matter, and released from subjection to the
body. Such a soul is called virgin. And she has for spouse,
not matter—for that she has renounced—but the Divine Spirit
which is God. And the man born of this union is in the
image of God, and is God made man; that is, he is Christ,
and it is the Christ thus born in every man, who redeems
him and endows him with eternal life." And from the same
source: "For, as cannot be too clearly and forcibly stated,
between the man who becomes a Christ, and other men,
there is no difference whatever of kind. The difference is
alone of condition and degree, and consists in difference of
unfoldment of the spiritual nature possessed by all in virtue
of their common derivation. 'All things,' as has repeatedly
been said, 'are made of the divine Substance.' And
Humanity represents a stream which, taking its rise in the
outermost and lowest mode of differentiation of that
Substance, flows inwards and upwards to the highest, which

is God. And the point at which it reaches the celestial, and empties itself into Deity, is 'Christ.' Any doctrine other than this—any doctrine which makes the Christ of a different and nonhuman nature—is anti-Christian and sub-human. And, of such doctrine, the direct effect is to cut off man altogether from access to God, and God from access to man."

NO SHORTCUTS

And from Basil Wilberforce, **Problems**: "In the evolution of God's life in man there are no short cuts, but a gradual unfolding of a principle of interior vitality. And the motto from this thought is, 'Rest in the Lord and wait patiently for Him,' while the child-Christ nature within you 'increases in wisdom and stature, and in favour with God and man.'"

J. Brierley, in his book **Studies of the Soul**, says: "God as the Absolute can, in the nature of things, only come into contact with man by a self limitation . . . In Christ, to begin with, we have a revelation of the Absolute in the limited. In Him, as the Church all along has joyfully confessed, we see God."

"The second coming of Christ is a symbol of the completion of the process of purification and development of the souls of humanity, when the lower of consciousness rises to union with the higher." From **Mystical Religions**, and quoting from Luke, "And then shall they see the Son of man coming in a cloud with power and great glory. But when these things begin to come to pass, look up, and lift up your heads; because your redemption draweth nigh."

R. M. Jones goes on to say: "This refers to the consummation of the physical at the end of the cycle. Then as perfection of the soul-state approaches, the indwelling Christ appears in glory within the souls of the saints, or is raised above the condition wherefrom at first his descent was made.

The 'cloud' signifies a temporary veil which obscures the splendour of the Highest. The 'lifting up of heads' refers to the aspiration of the minds, needful so that liberation from the lower nature may be effected." And quoting from Luke again, "Verily I say unto you, this generation shall not pass away, till all things be accomplished," he explains: "Christ here points out that each grade of evolution of qualities now existent, shall not be extinguished until the complete process of soul-growth on the lower planes has been carried out."

To return to our analysis of the Trinity—the Father is the Absolute, Unconditioned, First Cause; the Infinite Person; the Divine in Whom we live and move and have our being. The entire manifestation of the infinite in any and all planes, levels, states of consciousness, or manifestations, constitutes the Son.

THE BREATH OF GOD

So far as we know from teachings handed down to us from antiquity, the Holy Ghost signifies the feminine aspect of the Divine Trinity. It represents the divine activity of the higher mental plane; the Breath of God, or the Law of Being. It is difficult for us to transpose the meaning of ancient symbols into modern language, but it seems to be the consensus among the scholars who have studied this subject that the Holy Ghost means the relationship between the Father and the Son, or the divine, creative fertility of the universal soul when impregnated by the Divine Ideas. If creation is to take place, there must be a Divine Imagination which is spontaneous, and a creative medium through which It acts. This creative medium is the Law of Mind.

When any individual recognizes his or her true union with the Infinite, that individual automatically becomes the

Christ. The person is borne from the lower to a higher plane and awakes to a greater consciousness of his or her union with the Father–"I shall be satisfied when I awake in thy likeness."

Science of Mind makes clear that there is a universal Law of Mind which receives the impress of our thought and acts upon it. This Law is not God, but the servant of God.

The ancients called this Law the "Feminine." Realizing that there must be an active, energizing principle which is God, the Masculine, they also recognized that there must be a creative principle in nature, which they spoke of as Feminine, whose business it is to receive God's thought and bring it into creation.

THE CREATIVE LAW

This creative Law is, of course, the Law of Mind. It is what we mean when we say there is a Universal Mind through which the Universal Spirit operates. In other words, when we think of God as pure, self-knowing Spirit, as "our Father which art in heaven," as the Absolute, the Unconditioned, as Infinite Person and Limitless Being, we are thinking of Divine Intelligence. But when we think of the universe as Law, we are thinking of the Principle of Mind which receives the impress of our thought and acts upon it, always creatively, always mathematically, and without any respect to persons.

All great spiritual teachings have proclaimed such a creative Principle. It has been called by a thousand names, but careful analysis will show that every scripture has differentiated between God the Spirit and God the Law.

The ancients said that Spirit is the Power that knows Itself. They also taught the karmic law, which is the medium for all thought and action. Karma means the fruit of action.

When Jesus said, "The words that I speak unto you, they are spirit, and they are life," he was speaking from the consciousness of Christ which dominates the mental plane. His mind was such a perfect transmitter that it reflected, imaged, emanated or automatically became an instrument through which the Divine worked.

Knowing that his word was in absolute accord with Divine Harmony, he found no difference between it and the Word of God. It was his implicit confidence in his Divine inspiration, arrived at through a lifetime of contemplation and of conscious union with the Infinite, which gave him the confidence to say, ". . . till all these things be fulfilled. Heaven and earth shall pass away, but my words shall not pass away." Jesus was relying upon the Law of Mind to execute his word.

SPIRIT AND MIND

In the Science of Mind we are very careful to draw a distinction between Universal Spirit and Universal Mind. We know that in such degree as we inwardly realize the Truth, this Truth which we realize, operating through a universal Law of Mind, will find outward or physical manifestation in the world of form. This is what we mean when we say that the Spirit operates through a Law of Mind; that we are surrounded by this Mind, which receives the impress of our thought and acts upon it.

Let us see what different scriptures have had to say on this subject, starting with our own **Bible**. "In the beginning was the Word, and the Word was with God, and the Word was God." "Forever, O Lord, thy word is seated in heaven." "And, Thou, Lord . . . hast laid the foundation of the earth; and the heavens are the works of thine hands." "Our God is a living God. His power fills the universe . . . with his spirit thou breathest."

In referring to the Law of Mind the Bible says: "Every idle word that men shall speak, they shall give account thereof . . . for by thy words thou shalt be justified, and by thy words thou shalt be condemned." "And they were astonished at his doctrine: for his word was with power." "Be ye doers of the word and not hearers only . . ." "For there are three that bear witness in heaven, the Father, the Word, and the Holy Ghost: and these three are one."

Our Bible is based on the premise that God is pure Spirit; that He creates through the power of His word, and that the universe is a manifestation of His imagination (His imaging within Himself through knowing Himself to be what He is). God is Spirit. The Spirit speaks, the Law is invoked, and a manifestation necessarily takes form. This is the first principle.

THE SPIRITUAL IMAGE

The next principle is that we are the spiritual image and likeness of God, and are of like nature with God; that we are made of the essence of God, and are individualized centers in the Consciousness of God.

The Bible, then, having stated our divine pedigree, and having carefully pointed out what happens to us through our misuse of the Law of Freedom, commonly called "the fall of humankind," devotes its conclusion to man's redemption. The old prophets intuitively perceived this; the New Testament demonstrates it, for in the person of Jesus there arose a man who became so conscious of his union with good that all evil disappeared from his imagination.

Through trial, temptation, suffering, through success and

failure, this glorified soul, in a sense, fought the battle of life for all of us and thus automatically became the savior of humankind. But when they mistook the man Jesus for the Christ Principle, the wisdom of Jesus caused him to withdraw himself that the Spirit of Truth might awaken in them a corresponding realization of their own union with the Divine.

The whole teaching of the Bible may be simmered down to this simple statement, presented to each one of us individually as though a Divine Hand delivered it unto our individual keeping: *You are one with the creative Spirit of the universe.* There is a universal, divine Spirit which will inspire, guide, direct and companion you, but there is also a universal Law of Cause and Effect which sees to it that every act, every thought, every motive, must be accounted for. Finally, through suffering, you will learn to distinguish right from wrong; you will finally live in conscious union and in conscious communion with the Divine Spirit.

From then on, your words, thoughts and acts will be constructive and you will come into complete salvation. God has done all He can for you because He has delivered His entire nature into your keeping. But since this nature is truth, goodness, beauty, wisdom, love and power, you can never enter completely into the kingdom of harmony until you consciously unify with harmony.

A PERFECT BALANCE

This is the balance between truth and justice, between love and reason, between true divine freedom and the misuse of Law, which is not liberty but license. This is why Moses said, "I set before you this day a blessing and a curse; a blessing if ye obey the commandments . . . a curse, if ye will not obey the commandments."

The whole problem of evil, as stated by the different scriptures of the world, is not a problem of dealing with an entity of evil, but with the misuse of a dynamic power which, rightly used, alone guarantees freedom.

The **Koran** says that "whatsoever good betideth thee is from God and whatsoever betideth thee of evil is from thyself." And our **Bible** says of the Spirit, "Thou art of purer eyes than to behold evil, and canst not look on iniquity."

From the **Teachings of Buddha** we learn: "For the cause of the karma [cause and effect] which conducts to unhappy states of existence, is ignorance." "Therefore it is clear that ignorance can only be removed by wisdom." The **Zend-Avesta** says, "The word of falsehood smites but the word of truth shall smite it." And from **The Book of the Dead**: "It shall come to pass that the evil one shall fall when he raiseth a snare to destroy thee . . ."

From the **Text of Taoism** we learn: "Whatever is contrary to the Tao soon ends." "He who injures others is sure to be injured by them in return."

Healing the Sick

We believe in the healing of the sick through the power of this Mind.

Spiritual mind healing has long since passed the experimental stage, and we now know why faith has performed miracles. We live in a universe of pure, unadulterated Spirit, of perfect Being. We are, as Emerson said, in the lap of an infinite Intelligence. There is a spiritual prototype of perfection at the center of everything. There is a cosmic or Divine pattern at the center of every organ of the physical body. Our body is some part of the Body of God; it is a manifestation of the Supreme Spirit.

In the practice of spiritual mind healing we start with this simple proposition: God is perfect. God is all there is. God includes humankind. The spiritual person is a Divine being, as complete and perfect in essence as is God. When in thought, in contemplation, in imagination, in inward feeling, we consciously return to the Source of our being, the Divine pattern which already exists springs forth into newness of manifestation. When we clear the consciousness—that is, the whole mental life, both conscious and subjective—of discord, we are automatically healed.

A DEFINITE TECHNIQUE

The Science of Mind gives us a definite technique for doing this. It teaches us exactly how to proceed on a simple, understandable basis. It is a science because it is built upon the exact laws of Mind, for the laws of Mind are as exact as any other laws in nature. They are natural laws. From a practical viewpoint, this is done by making certain definite statements with the realization that they have power to remove any obstacle, to dissolve any false condition, and to reveal our spiritual nature.

True mind healing cannot be divorced from spiritual realization; therefore, the practitioner of this science must have a deep and an abiding sense of calm, of peace, and of his or her union with the Spirit. We must have an unshakable conviction that the spiritual person is perfect, that he or she is one with God, and we must know that in such degree as we realize, sense, or feel this inner perfection, it will appear. The physical healing itself is a result, an effect, of this inward consciousness.

The laws of this science are so simple, direct and usable that anyone may demonstrate them who cares to make the effort. Read carefully the entire section on mind healing in our textbook, *The Science of Mind*, and you will discover that there is no mystery about this. The reason that throughout the ages people have been healed through a prayer of faith is that faith complies with the Law of Mind in producing an affirmative result. Faith is an unquestioned acceptance.

THE NECESSITY OF FAITH

Faith also is a certain definite mental attitude. When Jesus said, "It is done unto you as you believe," he implied that a Law, a Force or an intelligent Energy in the universe acts upon the images of our belief. Faith is an affirmative way of using this Law, this Energy, this Force. Therefore, all scriptures announce the necessity of having faith.

"Be ye transformed by the renewing of your mind." "Be renewed in the spirit of your mind." "Let this mind be in you which was also in Christ." "I will put my laws into your mind." "Hear, O earth, behold I will bring evil upon these people, even the fruits of their thoughts." "And he sent his word and healed them." "He forgetteth all thine iniquities; he healeth all thy diseases." "O Lord, my God, I cry unto thee and thou hast healed me." "Then shall thy light break forth as the morning, and thine health shall spring forth speedily." "And it shall come to pass, that before they call, I will answer; and while they are yet speaking, I will hear." "I will take sickness away from the midst of thee." "The tongue of the wise is health." "Behold I will bring health . . . I will cure them . . ."

"Jesus turned him about, and when he saw her, he said, Daughter, be of good comfort; thy faith hath made thee whole. And the woman was made whole from that hour." "Then touched he their eyes, saying, According to your faith be it unto you. And their eyes were opened." "Heal the sick, cleanse the lepers, raise the dead, cast out devils: freely ye have received, freely give." "And great multitudes followed

him, and he healed them all." "And the blind and the lame
came to him in the temple, and he healed them."

In spiritual mind healing, thought becomes a transmitter
for Divine Power; therefore, the thought must always be
kept free from confusion.

HEALING IN OTHER TRADITIONS

It is interesting to note that, while all the great scriptures
of the ages concur about the nature of God and of
humankind, and the relationship between the spiritual and
the physical, outside the Christian scriptures very little is
mentioned about healing or the control of conditions
through the use of Divine Power, although they all agree that
when the mind reflects the Divine Perfection, healing and
prosperity follow.

In the **Text of Taoism** we find: "The still mind . . . is the
mirror of heaven and earth . . ." "Maintain a perfect unity in
every movement of your will. You will not wait for the hearing of your ears, but for the hearing of your mind. You will
not wait even for the hearing of your mind, but for the hearing of the Spirit." "Purity and stillness give the correct law to
all under heaven."

And from the **Koran**: "The Lord of the worlds He hath
created me and guideth me; He giveth me food and drink
and when I am sick He healeth me." "And never Lord have
I prayed to thee with ill success."

Jesus, the last of his particular line of prophets, was the
first to introduce spiritual mind healing and definitely to
instruct his followers to practice it. People have been healed
through all faiths, but the great healing shrines of the
Christian belief have undoubtedly emphasized this more
than most others, although we do find many instances of
healing through all the various beliefs.

THE "NEW THOUGHT" MOVEMENT

More particularly since the advent of what has been called "The New Thought," which started in America and has since spread throughout the world, do we find great emphasis placed upon spiritual healing.

This has been a sincere, earnest and effective attempt to get back to some of the first principles which Jesus taught. He sent out his disciples, telling them to heal the sick as a proof, not only of their Divine Power, but also of their Divine Authority, and he said, "Lo, I am with you alway." Since it is self-evident that Jesus, as a human being, could not be with them always, common sense compels us to accept that when he said, "I am with you alway," he was referring to the Divine Power, the Christ Principle, which he used.

To speak of the *science* of Jesus is no misnomer, for he certainly knew what he was doing, and repeatedly stated that his words acted as spiritual law. It might be said of Jesus that he was a practical idealist. He did not believe that the Kingdom of God is some far-off event; to him it was an ever-present reality; it was always at hand waiting merely to be perceived by the inner spiritual intuition, which is the voice of God operating through humankind.

"Faith without works is dead." Therefore, faith should be justified through manifestation, and if we have faith we can scientifically prove this. For, after all, science is the knowledge of universal principles and laws consciously applied for definite purposes.

WHY IT IS A SCIENCE

There is a science of Mind and Spirit because there is a principle of Mind and Spirit. There is a possibility of using this science because we now understand how the laws of Mind and Spirit work in human affairs. The Principle of Mind operates through our thought, through our faith and conviction, and, most effectively, through an attitude of love, of compassion and of sympathy constructively used. It is impossible to make the highest use of the laws of Mind without basing such use of these laws upon inward spiritual perception, upon a conscious realization of our union with God.

When the physician and the metaphysician come better to understand each other they will more closely cooperate. It is self-evident that each is seeking to alleviate human suffering. No intelligent person would deny the need of physicians, surgeons and hospitals. On the other hand, it is generally agreed that a large percentage of our physical troubles are mental in their origin, and that all have some relationship to mental processes. It is most important, then, that the work of the sincere metaphysician be both understood and appreciated.

It is not at all probable that the psychologist can take the place of the metaphysician, for just as the mere healing of the body, without an adjustment of the mental and emotional states, is insufficient, so the adjusting of mental and emotional states without introducing spiritual values will be ineffectual. Hence, there is an important place for the metaphysician, and his or her assistance should be sought.

Physician, metaphysician and psychologist should cooperate. There should be no sense of mistrust or criticism among them. The metaphysician should appreciate both the psychologist and the physician.

THE VALUE OF MEDICINE

In the early days of spiritual therapeutics it was believed that one could not treat people mentally with success if they were being attended by a physician, or if they were using material methods for relief. Now we know that this idea was based on superstition. We no longer give it any serious thought. The metaphysician feels it a privilege to be called into consultation with a physician or with a psychologist. He or she has learned to appreciate the field of medicine and surgery.

The day is certain to come when the field of medicine will recognize, appreciate, and cooperate with the metaphysical field. Even today this practice is far more common than the average person realizes. (When the metaphysician stops making foolish statements denying that the patient is ill, he or she will find a greater inclination toward recognition from the medical world.)

Today most physicians recognize the power of thought in relation to the body. All realize the dynamic energy of the emotions. Just as psychology and psychiatry are being introduced into the medical world, so the metaphysical gradually will be understood, accepted and appreciated. Already many psychologists are affirming the necessity of introducing spiritual values into their practice. Who is going to meet this need unless it be the metaphysician?

Progress is inevitable and cooperation between all right-minded workers in the healing arts is certain. Let us do all that we can to remove superstition, intolerance and bigotry, which after all merely result in stupidity. We should unite in one common cause, not only to alleviate physical suffering but, insofar as possible, to remove its cause. If much of this cause lies hidden in the realm of mind, then surely those who are equipped to work in this realm are contributing their share to the meeting of a human need.

Controlling Conditions

We believe in the control of conditions through the power of this Mind.

While all sacred writings affirm that when we are in harmony with the Infinite we are automatically prospered, the Christian scriptures lay greater stress on prosperity through spiritualizing the mind than any other of the bibles of the world. Our Bible, truly understood, is a book for the emancipation of humankind from the thralldom of every evil, every lack and limitation.

From the teaching of Moses, running through the thought of the major prophets and culminating in the brilliant manifestation of the Mind of the Christ through the thought of Jesus, over and over this idea is reiterated—that if we live in harmony with the Spirit everything we do shall prosper.

The Science of Mind teaches that through right knowledge, we may definitely and consciously demonstrate (that is, prove or show forth) practical results of spiritual thought. Countless thousands have proved this principle and there is no longer any question about its effectiveness.

The greatest guide we have for this is found in the inspired writings of the Christian scriptures. "Prove me now herewith, saith the Lord of hosts, if I will not open you the windows of heaven, and pour you out a blessing, that there shall not be room enough to receive it." "And he shall pray unto God and he will be favorable unto him." "For every one that asketh receiveth; and he that seeketh findeth; and to him that knocketh it shall be opened." "Ask, and it shall be given you." "And all things, whatsoever ye shall ask in prayer, believing, ye shall receive."

BELIEVE AND RECEIVE

Whether we choose to call this faith or understanding makes no difference. It really is faith based upon understanding; it is belief elevated to the mental position of unconditioned certainty. For Jesus said that whoever could believe ". . . and shall not doubt in his heart, but shall believe that those things which he saith shall come to pass; he shall have whatsoever he saith. Therefore I say unto you, What things soever ye desire, when ye pray, believe that ye receive them, and ye shall have them."

Nothing could be more definite or concise than this statement. We must actually believe that there is a Power, an Intelligence, a Law, which will make this desire manifest in our experience.

There is a Law of Mind which follows the patterns of our thought. This Law works automatically. It will always respond by corresponding. Thus Jesus said that it is done unto us *as* we believe. The word *as* is important since it implies that the creative Intelligence, in working *for* us, must work *through* us at the level of our acknowledgment of It as working. This is working *in spirit and in truth,* and according to Law. And there must be law even in prayer, if there is to be cosmic order.

SURRENDERING THE INTELLECT

Our human mind has been likened to the "Workshop of God," for it is here that the tools of thought consciously may fashion destiny, may carve out a new future.

We have been told to do this according to the pattern shown us on the Mount. This means that we are to formulate our ideas on the premise that there is an all-sustaining Power and an all-pervading Presence around us, and an immutable Law ever serving us when our lives are in harmony with the Divine Nature. Through an exact law, demonstration follows the word of faith. This calls for a surrender of the intellect to a spiritual conviction which dares to believe, disregarding any evidence to the contrary.

We must continue in faith until our whole mental life, both conscious and subjective, responds. If we would pray and prosper we must believe that the Spirit is both willing and able to make the gift. But since the Spirit can only give us what we take, and since the taking is a mental act, we must train the mind to believe and to accept. This is the secret of the power of prayer.

We need not have great intellectual attainment to understand these simple things. Jesus said that the Kingdom of Heaven is reached through childlike faith. Again he said, "I thank thee, O Father . . . because thou hast hid these things from the wise and the prudent, and hast revealed them unto babes."

Just as the teachings of Jesus announce the Divine Presence, so his works prove the presence of a Law which received the impress of his word and brought it forth into form. He asked no authority other than that which was demonstrated through his act. Since Jesus taught the most definite system of spiritual thought ever given to the world, as well as the most simple and direct, and since he was able to prove his teaching by his works, we could do no better than to follow his example. There are two ways in which we may do this. One is blind faith (and we cannot doubt its effectiveness); the other is through coming to understand what the teachings of Jesus really meant. Thus knowledge passes into a faith so complete that it is unshakable.

EXPLICIT INSTRUCTIONS

Jesus left very explicit instructions relative to prayer. He said, "Judge not according to appearances." That is, do not be confused by the conditions around you. This is the first great instruction of Jesus—to have such faith and confidence in the Invisible that appearances no longer disturb you.

Next we come to the preparation for prayer. Having shut out all appearances to the contrary, enter the closet. To enter the closet means to withdraw into your own thought, to shut out all confusion and discord. Here in the silence of the soul, look to the all-creative Wisdom and Power, to the ever-present Substance. When we have entered the closet and shut the door to outward appearances, we next make known our requests—"what things soever ye desire."

Next Jesus tells us that we are to *believe that we actually possess* the objects of our desire, disregarding all appearances to the contrary. We are to enter into this invisible inheritance acting as though it were true. Our faith in the substance of the Invisible is to take actual form. The Divine Giver Himself is to make the gift, but first we must believe that we have received it, and then we shall receive it—". . . believe that ye receive them, and ye shall have them."

This is a veiled statement of the Law of Cause and Effect operating in human affairs. When we have believed that we have, we have actually given birth to the form that is to be presented. Having made known our request with thanksgiving and received the answer with gratitude, we must rest assured that the Law will bring about the desired result.

"Thy Father which seeth in secret himself shall reward thee openly." Rest in peace knowing that it is done. This profound principle which Jesus announced (and the simple technique of its use in which he counselled his followers) exists today in all of its fullness. It is the very cornerstone upon which our philosophy is built.

Even in Divine communion we deal with the Law of Cause and Effect. Our prayer invokes this Divine Law and causes It to manifest in our external world at the level of our inner perception of Its working. Because this is true, prayer should always be definite, conscious and active.

"BEFORE THEY CALL . . ."

Prayer ties us to a Power that is able, ready and willing to fulfill every legitimate desire; to bring every good thing to us; to do for us even more abundantly than we have expected. "Before they call, I will answer; and while they are yet speaking, I will hear." This shifting of the burden is important, for when we feel isolated, alone and struggling against tremendous odds, we are not equal to the task before us. Life becomes a drudgery rather than a *jubilant beholding*. But if we know the burden is lifted and set upon the shoulders of the Law, then power and speed come to hands and feet; joy floods the imagination with anticipation.

The reflection of an image in a mirror is an exact likeness of the image which is held before the mirror. So the Law of Cause and Effect reflects back to us a likeness of the image of our thought. Thus we are told that we reflect the glory of God. But too often we reflect the fear and limitation of humankind rather than the glory of God.

We must find new meanings to life if we hope to create new images which, in their turn, will supply new reflections. Jesus told us to judge not according to appearances but to judge righteously. If we judge only according to what is now transpiring, our reflection of these images will merely perpetuate the old limitation; but if we judge righteously, that is, if we look to the omnipotence of Good, we shall create new images of thought which will reflect greater abundance.

PRAYER IS A MIRROR

Prayer, then, is a mirror reflecting the images of our thought through the Law of Good into our outward experiences. But are we reflecting the glory of God or the confusion of humankind? Jesus carefully pointed out that before we can reach a position of absolute power, we must first have complied with the Law of Love. For the whole impulsion of the universe is an impulsion of Love, the manifestation of Divine Givingness.

The Apostle Paul said, "I will pray with the spirit and I will pray with the understanding also . . ." This is an instruction for us to combine spiritual intuition with definite mental acceptance. He is telling us to use the gift of God consciously.

We are also told to pray without ceasing, to maintain a steadfast conviction, disregarding every apparent contradiction, obstruction or appearance that would deny the good we affirm. "But let him ask in faith, nothing wavering. For he that wavereth is like a wave of the sea driven with the wind and tossed." "To the righteous good shall be repaid." "The minds of the righteous shall stand." "Behold the righteous shall be recompensed in the earth." "The righteous man is delivered of all trouble." A righteous person is one who is right with the universe; one who lives in accord with the Divine Will and the Divine Nature; one who lives in harmony with good.

We have the right then to expect, and we should expect, insofar as our inner thought is in tune with the Infinite, that everything we do shall prosper.

Life Loves and Gives

We believe in the eternal Goodness, the eternal Loving-Kindness,
and the eternal Givingness of Life to all.

The Spirit gives Itself to everyone; the Power of God is delivered to all. "Whosoever will may come." No matter what the mistakes of our yesterdays may have been, we may transcend both the mistake and its consequence through imbibing the Spirit of Truth, which is the Power of God.

This does not mean that we may continue living in the mistake without suffering from it. We must transcend it. That is, we must transmute hate into love, fear into faith and a sense of separation into conscious union with good. When we have done this, the entire record of the past is blotted out

and we are again free—freed with that freedom which the
Almighty has ordained, and which we may claim as our
own.

But liberty is not license and the Law of Life cannot be
fooled. It is exact and exacting. "Therefore," Jesus said, "all
things whatsoever ye would that men should do unto you,
do ye even so to them." "Give, and it shall be given."

This is a statement of the Law of Cause and Effect, which
is invariable and immutable, but which is also the plaything
both of God and humankind, for while the Law Itself cannot
be broken, any particular sequence of cause and effect in It
can be transcended. The same law which brought poverty,
sickness and death, rightly used will bring peace, wholeness,
prosperity and life.

THE CHALLENGE OF FAITH

This is the great challenge of spiritual faith. The Christian
philosophy bids us not to look with doleful introspection on
previous errors; but coming daily to the Fountain of Life to
be renewed in mind, thought and spirit, we shall find that we
also are renewed in bodily conditions and in physical affairs.

The Scripture boldly declares the triumph of the Spirit of
Christ over all evil: Be ye transformed by the renewing of
your mind; by the putting off of the old person and the
putting on of the new person, which is Christ. "Lo, I am with
you alway, even unto the end of the world."

14 Our Life Is God's Life

We believe in our own soul, our own spirit and our own destiny;
for we understand that the life of all is God.

We are not only centers of God Consciousness; we are immortal beings, forever expanding, forever spiraling upward, forever growing in spiritual stature. Not *some* people, but *all* people are immortal, for everyone will finally overcome or transcend any misuse of the Law which we have made in his ignorance. Complete redemption at last must come alike to all.

What transformations must ensue, what changes of consciousness must take place before this is finally brought about, the finite has not yet grasped; but through the whisperings of Divine intuition we know that even though we now see as through a glass darkly, we shall someday behold Reality face to face. We shall be satisfied when we consciously awake in the likeness of that Divinity which shapes our ends.

"Beloved, now are we the sons of God, and it doth not yet appear what we shall be: but we know that, when he shall appear, we shall be like him; for we shall see him as he is." We are all in the process of spiritual evolution, but there is certainty behind us, certainty before us and certainty with us at every moment. The Eternal Light will break through wherever we permit It to.

Potentially, everything that is to be, exists now; but our spiritual vision has not yet become completely in tune with the Infinite. This is the high task set before us; this is the deathless hope implanted in our mind by the Divine.

The trials and troubles of human experience; the blind groping of the finite toward the Infinite; the sickness, poverty, death, uncertainty, fear and doubt that accompany us constitute the cross upon which we must offer, as a sacrifice to our ignorance, that which does not belong to the Kingdom of Good. But from this cross something triumphant will emerge, for as Emerson said, "The finite alone has wrought and suffered; the infinite lies stretched in smiling repose."

Shall we not, then, go forth with joy to meet the new day, endeavoring so to embody the Spirit of Christ that the Divine in us shall rise triumphant, resurrected, to live forever in the City of God? More could not be asked than that which the Divine has already delivered; less should not be expected.

Appendix

WHAT ARE THE SOURCES
WE HAVE QUOTED?

Professor Max Muller, one of the greatest European Orientalists and author of *The Sacred Books of the East*, has well said that "the true religion of the future will be the fulfillment of all the religions of the past. . . . All religions, so far as I know them, had the same purpose; all were links in a chain which connects heaven and earth; and which is held, and always was held, by one and the same hand. All here on earth tends toward right and truth, and perfection; nothing here on earth can ever be quite right, quite true, quite perfect, not even Christianity—or what is called Christianity—so long as it excludes all other religions, instead of loving and embracing what is good in each."

Like many other religions of antiquity, the origin of
Taoism is more or less obscure. According to some
authorities it is said to have begun around 600 B.C. (which
antedates Confucius, who was born in 551 B.C.). The world
generally associates **Taoism** with Lao-Tze, a Chinese metaphysical philosopher who was fifty-three years older than
Confucius. It was this philosopher who must have gathered
together these teachings. Archdeacon Hardwick tells us that
the Chinese word *Tao* ". . . was adopted to denominate an
abstract cause, or the initial principle of life and order, to
which worshippers were able to assign the attribute of imma-
teriality, eternity, immensity, invisibility."

The **Upanishads**, the **Vedas**, the **Mahabharata**, the
Raja Yoga philosophy, as well as the **Bhagavad-Gita**, are all
drawn from the ancient wisdom of India.

The philosophy of **Buddha**, who was born in the sixth
century B.C., is well enough known not to need any
comment.

The Sacred Book of the Parsis is called the **Zend-Avesta**,
which is a collection of fragments of ideas that prevailed in
ancient Persia, five years before the Christian era and for
several centuries afterwards.

The Book of the Dead is a series of translations of the
ancient Egyptian hymns and religious texts. They were
found on the walls of tombs, in coffins and in papyri. Like
many other sacred traditions, there probably were no written
copies in the earlier days; they were committed to memory
and handed down from generation to generation.

Some students believe that the books of **Hermes
Trismegistus**, which means "the thrice greatest," originally
derived from ancient Egyptian doctrine. Hermes was a
Greek god, son of Zeus and Maia, daughter of Atlas. To

Hermes was attributed the authorship of all the strictly sacred books generally called by Greek authors **Hermetic.** According to some scholars, the Egyptian Hermes "was a symbol of the Divine Mind; he was the incarnated Thought, the living Word—the primitive type of the Logos of Plato and the Word of the Christians. . . ."

Fragments of a Faith Forgotten are taken from the Gnostics, those "who used the Gnosis as the means to set their feet upon the Way of God." Gnosticism was pre-Christian and originated in the ancient religion and philosophy of the Greeks, the Egyptians and the Jews.

According to H. Polano, the **Talmud** contains ". . . the thoughts . . . of a thousand years of the national life of the Jewish people."

The **Koran** is the sacred book of the Mohammedans, consisting of revelations orally delivered at intervals by Mohammed and collected in writing after his death. The **Koran** is considered one of the most important of the world's sacred books.

The **Apocrypha** refers to a collection of ancient writings. The Greek word "Apocryphos" was originally used about books, the contents of which were kept hidden or secret because they embodied the special teachings of religious or philosophical sects; only the members of these sects were initiated into the secrets of this teaching.

IV

A Science of Religion and a Religion of Science

How science and spirituality, once believed to be antagonists, are coming together.

A Science of Religion
and a Religion of Science

There are three general classifications of knowledge—namely, science, philosophy and religion. By *science* we mean the organized knowledge of natural law and its application to life. By *philosophy* we mean the opinions we hold about the world, life and reality. Although we generally speak of philosophy in relation to those statements which have been put down in writing by people whose opinions we respect, as a matter of fact philosophy is anybody's opinion about anything. By *religion* we mean any person's belief about his or her relationship to the invisible universe. Or we might say, religion is humankind's idea of God or gods—of the ultimate reality.

LAWS OR OPINIONS?

It follows, then, that there are many philosophies and many religions, since in both instances they constitute opinions. But not so with science, for science is a knowledge of the laws of nature. A scientist, in whatever field of investigation he or she may be engaged, is one who uses universal principles. Once a principle is discovered and the laws governing it are ascertained, the scientist maintains absolute faith in that principle.

Science is not an investigation into the why, but into the how. Science makes no attempt to answer the why of anything, that is, the reason for its being. (If it should shift its field from knowledge of principles and facts into the field of inquiry as to why these principles exist, then science becomes philosophy.)

Today, many people of science are beginning to speculate more deeply on scientific principles. And as they do this, their speculations fall into two generalized philosophical classifications. These speculations usually lead them either to a philosophic basis of *materialism* or to a philosophic basis of *idealism*.

Both the idealist and the materialist believe that the universe is a thing of intelligence. The only difference is that the materialist refuses to admit that the intelligence operating through the laws of nature is backed by or permeated with any form of consciousness; that is, the intelligence is merely a blind but intelligent force, a conglomeration of immutable laws of cause and effect with no element of consciousness, no sentiment, no feeling. Materialists see only blind force, but they see blind force intelligently organized.

The idealist, however, feels that back of and operating in and through the laws of nature is volition and consciousness.

The idealist maintains that the manifestation of physical life upon this planet always is in accord with organized intelligence, and also feels that organized intelligence can be accounted for only on the basis that there is an Engineer as well as an Engine.

There are, then, these two branches of philosophy—the idealistic and the materialistic. The idealist believes in consciousness, hence a Spiritual Universe, while the materialist does not.

THE BIG DIFFERENCE

Naturally, the scientist who is philosophically a materialist believes in no God, no Spiritual Universe and no consciousness in the Universe which responds to humankind. This scientist does not believe in the immortality of the individual soul, nor can he or she give any real meaning to life. This scientist may be a humanitarian and a very good person, but his or her ultimate philosophy is: "Six feet under and all is over."

The scientist who feels that the universe *has* a consciousness finds no difficulty in believing in God or in the universe as a spiritual system, permeated with a consciousness which responds to humankind. Therefore this scientist believes in prayer, immortality and the value of faith, and feels there is a definite meaning to life. An increasing number of scientific people are taking this position.

But if the idealist is a scientific person, believing as he or she must that everything is governed by law, the idealist's religion cannot be superstitious. The idealist cannot believe in a God who specializes for one person more than for another, or who has esteem for one person above another; nor can he or she believe that the laws of nature can be broken or modified through anyone's prayer or faith. Therefore the scientific mind which is at the same time idealistic believes that the universe is not only intelligent, but that it is also consciousness, and this scientist will be satisfied with no religious concepts which contradict reason, common sense and a cosmos of law and order.[1]

A RETURN TO SPIRITUALITY

When the early discoveries of science refuted ancient superstitions and proved that this world was not the center of the universe, that it was round and not flat, many people's faith began to wane. Intelligent people could no longer hold the ancient shibboleths, dogmas and superstitions valid and formalized religion began losing its hold on the inquiring scientific mind. Materialism was ascending.

However, today we find increasing numbers of scientific men and women emerging from that age of materialism. This is because modern science has not theoretically been able to resolve the material universe into purely mechanical energy, but has discovered that the smallest particles which it supposes to exist exercise a sort of volition, which of course leaves room for freedom.[2] Once you establish freedom and volition as an operating factor in connection with the energy which becomes form,[3] then you have established a universe of consciousness. And once you establish a universe of consciousness you establish the possibility of communion, and arrive at a logical basis for faith, prayer and the religious and the mystical life.

A tremendous growth of knowledge has taken place in the world in the last few hundred years. However, the vast majority of people have given but little thought to the implications involved. To most people religion has been either superstitiously entertained—and no doubt with great benefit to those who believed in it—or else it was rejected.

But today, there is a certain and rather swift return to spiritual convictions. These new, vital and dynamic spiritual concepts have placed firm foundations beneath our innate religious tendency, firm foundations which scientific people need not reject and which the unscientific person may accept without superstition.[4]

This is what we mean by scientific religion. We do not mean that religion is reduced to coldness, without sentiment or feeling, but rather that law and order are added to the sentiment and the feeling. We have a perfect right to speak of a scientific religion or a religion of science. But upon what could such a scientific religion be based? It could only be based upon the principle of Mind, of Intelligence and Consciousness, which many outstanding scientists today assert is the ultimate and fundamental reality.

Science, in affirming consciousness in the universe (that is, a spiritual Presence and an Intelligence), also affirms that the individual's consciousness is of similar nature.[5] Therefore a scientific religion does not exclude what we call prayer or communion, even though it lays greater stress on communion than on petition. For instance, a scientific religion could not believe that our petitions to God can change the natural order of the universe or reverse the laws of nature.

However, prayer now becomes the communion of the lesser with the greater, which makes it possible for us, not to reverse natural law, but to reverse our *position* in it in such a way that bondage becomes freedom.[6]

A RELIGIOUS SCIENCE

We might speak of a pure religious science as we would speak of a pure natural science, which means the study of natural causes. We might speak of pure religious science as that branch of science which studies natural principles; the nature of Mind and Consciousness. Then we could think of applied religious science as the application of this principle to human needs for practical purposes, and this is where we encounter the study of prayer, of faith and of mental actions and reactions.

In the use of faith, prayer, communion or spiritual treatment, we apply the principles of Mind, Spirit, Intelligence, Consciousness and Law and Order to the problems of everyday life. By doing so, we would, then, be more than a theoretical religionist; we would have an applied and a practical religion.

This is exactly what we mean when we speak of a science of religion and a religion of science, for we use this term in its broadest sense. We use the term "religion" from the standpoint of universal religion, including all religious beliefs— Christian, Buddhist, Mohammedan or any other faith—and we think of prayer, communion and the laws of consciousness as applied to any and all people. In short, we universalize the Principle which by nature is universal. Thus each religion approaches the same God and must basically believe in the same God. But a scientific religion cannot believe in any concept of God which denies a universe of law and order, or which attempts to exclude anyone from its benefits.

It would be unscientific as well as irrational to believe that God, or the Supreme Intelligence, holds one person in higher esteem than another. For as the Bible so truthfully and boldly declares: "And let him that is athirst come. And whosoever will, let him take the water of life freely."

ALL'S LOVE—ALL'S LAW

One comes to agree with Robert Browning that "all's love, yet all's law," and that there is an impersonal Law as well as a personal relationship to the Spirit. This Law exists for all, like the laws of mathematics or any other natural law, but the relationship is personified through each individual at the level of his or her consciousness, at the level of each person's comprehension of what God means to him or her.

Intelligence and reason must be the rules of thought, and God must be accessible to all on equal terms. The scientific religionist cannot believe in miracles, but he or she will not deny the power of spiritual thought. Rather the scientific religionist will think that the so-called miracles performed as a result of spiritual faith have been in accord with natural law and cosmic order, and that they can be reproduced at will. That which the illumined have experienced and that which persons of great spiritual power have proved, the scientific religionist feels can be deliberately used in everyday life.

To the individual believing there is a Principle, Intelligence or Consciousness governing all things, there comes a feeling that he or she understands the laws, or at least some of the laws, of this Principle; hence the person feels that it is intensely sane as well as humanly practical to apply faith, consciousness and spiritual conviction to the solution of human problems. This is what is meant by spiritual mind treatment.

SPIRITUAL MIND TREATMENT

Spiritual mind treatment is based on the belief or the theory, which we now feel has a sound basis, that there is a Principle of Intelligence in the universe which is not only creative and gives rise to objective form, but is also immediately responsive to our consciousness. And, being universal, It is omnipresent; and being omnipresent, It is not only *where* we are but It is *what* we are.[7] Hence scientific religionists feel that they understand what Jesus meant when he said: "The words that I speak unto you I speak not of myself, but the Father, that dwelleth in me, he doeth the works."

Just as all pure science, before it can be useful to humanity, must pass into applied science, so pure religious concepts, before they can have a practical application, must pass into applied religion. And it is the application of religion to the solution of our problems which we may speak of as demonstrating the Principle.

What, then, are the pure and applied aspects of this Principle? The basis or pure concept is that there is an Absolute Intelligence in the universe—one, undivided, birthless, deathless, changeless Reality. Since no one made God and since God did not make Himself, that which was, is, and is to be, will remain.

After our first axiom (that God is all there is), is the implication that there is nothing else beside God. Hence the entire manifestation of Life is an evolution or an unfoldment of form from that which is formless and eternal. This intelligent Cause, this undifferentiated and undistributed God-Principle, one and complete with Itself, is the source from which all action proceeds and in which all creation takes place.

At this point one may logically hold the belief, the opinion or the certainty that God as us, in us, *is* us; that when we make a proclamation it is still God proclaiming, but at the level of our consciousness. Therefore the cosmos is reflected in, or manifested by or through, the individual. One cannot say, "Why is humankind?" any more than one can say,

"Why is God?" Intelligence exists and we interpret It. Therefore we are Its representative; we are personifications of the Infinite, governed by the same laws. But we are more than law; we are consciousness.

APPLYING THE PRINCIPLES

Applying the principles of such a science of religion to our everyday problems is just as necessary as practically applying the theories of any science. . . if they are to be of value. It is not enough merely to speculate or philosophize. It is certainly not enough to abstract our thought and simply announce an Infinite, for the Infinite can never at any time mean more to us than the use of It. This is true of any and all principles of nature.

If there is an infinite Creative Intelligence which makes things out of Itself by becoming the things that It makes, and if we exist and are conscious, then the Creative Genius of this Universal Mind is also the creative genius of Its individualization, which we call humankind.

From the above stated propositions intelligence cannot escape; correct induction and deduction cannot escape. Thus, most of the great intellectual geniuses who have ever lived have proclaimed these truths in their own tongues, in their own ways, in their own day, for their own age. Many believe that Jesus proclaimed these truths for all ages since he was so universal in his concepts.

Such a way of thinking does not belong to any sect, to any group, to any class, and most certainly not to any person. There is no claim to special revelation; rather, for this particular system of thought, facts from all ages and all people, from all philosophies and religions have been gathered together. And using practical methods which any other scientific research would use, this way of thinking is able to and does present to the world a Science of Mind with a message of freedom and enlightenment.

NOTES

[1] *"Religion and natural science are fighting a joint battle in an incessant, never relaxing crusade against skepticism and against dogmatism, against disbelief and against superstition, and the rallying cry in this crusade has always been, and always will be: 'On to God!'"*

–Max Planck

[2] *Heisenberg's Theory of Indeterminacy.*

[3] *Einstein's theory of the equivalence of energy and mass.*

[4] *"The idea that God . . . is not a being of caprice and whim, as had been the case in all the main body of thinking of the ancient world, but is instead a God who rules through law . . . That idea has made modern science and it is unquestionably the foundation of modern civilization."*

–Robert A. Millikan

[5] *". . . That consciousness is a singular of which the plural is unknown; that there is only one thing and that, which seems to be a plurality, is merely a series of different aspects of this one thing."*

–Erwin Schrodinger

[6] *"Prayer and propitiation may still influence the course of physical phenomena when directed to these centers."*

–Sir Arthur Eddington

[7] *"We discover that the universe shows evidence of a designing or controlling power that has something in common with our own individual minds."*

–Sir James Jeans

V

How to Give a Spiritual Mind Treatment

*Step-by-step instructions on how to use
the Science of Mind for your personal need.*

How to Give a
Spiritual Mind
Treatment

Take definite time at least twice each day to be alone, to sit down and compose your mind and think about God. Try to arrive at a deep sense of peace and calm. Then assume an attitude of faith in a Power greater than you are.

Next, say: *The words I speak are my law of good and they will produce the desired result because they are operated on by a Power greater than I am. Good alone goes from me and good alone returns to me.*

You are now ready to give a specific treatment for yourself. Begin by saying: *This word is for myself. Everything I say is for me and about me. It is the truth about my real self.* (You are thinking about your spiritual nature, the Divine Reality of yourself, the God in you.) Say: *There is One Life, that Life is God, that*

Life is perfect, that Life is my Life now. Say this slowly and with deep meaning.

Next, say: *My body is a manifestation of the living Spirit. It is created and sustained by the One Presence and the One Power. That Power is flowing in and through me now, animating every organ, every action, and every function of my physical being. There is perfect circulation, perfect assimilation and perfect elimination. There is no congestion, no confusion and no inaction. I am One with the infinite rhythm of Life which flows through me in love, in harmony and in peace. There is no fear, no doubt and no uncertainty in my mind. I am letting that Life which is perfect flow through me. It is my life now. There is One Life, that Life is God, that Life is perfect, that Life is my life now.* (In treating for particular conditions, use one of the specific affirmations which applies to your need.)

Next, deny everything that contradicts this. Follow each denial with a direct affirmation of its opposite. In a certain sense you are presenting a logical argument to your own mind, based on the belief that there is but one Life, which is perfect and which is your life now. The evidence that you bring out in your argument should reach a conclusion that causes your own mind to accept the verdict of perfection. Remember, you are not talking about your physical body as though it were separate from the Spirit, but about God in you. Therefore you will have no difficulty in convincing yourself that this God in you is perfect.

You have now reached a place of realization, where you enter into a feeling of assurance that comes from a consciousness of the Divine Presence in, around and through you. This period of realization should last for several moments during which you sit quietly, accepting the meaning of what you have said. Then, say: *It is now done. It is now complete. There is One Life, that Life is God, that Life is perfect, that Life is my life now.*

Between these periods of meditation try to keep your mind poised in such a way that you do not contradict what you have said in your treatment. Keep your mind open at all times to an influx of new inspiration, new power and new life. Accept what you have said with joy and gratitude.

Note: When treating another, say: *This word is for* . . . then say the person's name and continue exactly as though you were treating yourself.

SPECIFIC AFFIRMATIONS

RIGHT ACTION

Everything that I do, say or think is governed by Divine Intelligence and inspired by Divine Wisdom. I am guided into right action. I am surrounded with friendship, love and beauty. Enthusiastic joy, vitality and inspiration are in everything I do. I am conscious of Divine Guidance. I accept complete happiness, abundant health and increasing prosperity. I am aware of my partnership with the Infinite. I know that everything I do shall prosper.

HAPPINESS

Every thought of not being wanted, or of being afraid; every thought of uncertainty and doubt is cast out of my mind. I rely on God alone, in whom I live, move and have my being. A sense of happiness, peace and certainty flows through me. I have confidence in myself because I have confidence in God. I am sure of myself because I am sure of God.

PROBLEMS

The Spirit within me knows the answer to the problem which confronts me. I know that the answer is here and now. It is within my own mind because God is right where I am. I now turn from the problem to the Spirit, accepting the answer. In calm confidence, in perfect trust, in abiding faith and with complete peace, I let go of the problem and receive the answer.

SUCCESS

I know exactly what to do in every situation. Every idea necessary to successful living is brought to my attention. The doorway to ever-increasing opportunities for self-expression is open before me. I am continually meeting new and larger experiences. Every day brings some greater good. Every day brings more blessings and greater self-expression. I am prospered in everything I do. There is no deferment, no delay, no obstruction or obstacle to impede the progress of right action.

ABUNDANCE

I identify myself with abundance; I surrender all fear and doubt. I let go of all uncertainty. I know there is no confusion, no lack of confidence. The Presence of God is with me. The Mind of God is my mind. The Freedom of God is my freedom. The Power of God is my power. The Abundance of God fills my every good desire right now.

SECURITY

The Law of God is flowing through me. I am one with the rhythm of Life. There is nothing to be afraid of. There is nothing to be uncertain about. God is over all, in all and through all. God is right where I am. I am at peace with the world in which I live. I am at home with the Divine Spirit in which I am immersed.

LOVE

Today I bestow the essence of love upon everything. Everyone I meet shall be lovely to me. My soul meets the soul of the Universe in everyone. This love is a healing power touching everything into wholeness.

VI

Spiritual Mind
Treatments for
Personal Use

*Forty inspirational guides to solving problems and changing your life.
Followed by affirmations for specific application.*

Dissolve Obstacles and Wrong Conditions

Your knowledge that the great "I Am" is ever available gives you an increasing capacity to draw upon It, and to become inwardly aware of the presence of Spirit within you. Through the quiet contemplation of the omniaction of Spirit, learn to look quietly and calmly upon every false condition, seeing through it to the invisible side of Reality which molds conditions and re-creates all of your affairs closer to a Divine pattern.

With a penetrating spiritual vision you can dissipate the obstruction, remove the obstacle, dissolve the wrong condition.

SAY:

I now claim health instead of sickness, wealth instead of poverty, happiness instead of misery.

In such degree as I gain mastery over the sense of negation, whether it be pain or poverty, I am proving the Law of Mind in action.

Every thought of fear or limitation is removed from my consciousness.

I know that my word transmutes every energy into constructive action, producing health, harmony, happiness and success.

I know there is *something* at the center of my being which is absolutely certain of *itself*.

It has complete assurance, and *it* gives me complete assurance that all is well.

I maintain my position as a Divine Being, here and now.

Remove Blockages
from Your Life

You know that there is a God-Power at the center of every person's being, a Power that knows neither lack, limitation, fear, sickness, disquiet nor imperfection. But because you are an individual you can build a wall of negative thoughts between yourself and this perfection. The wall which keeps you from your greater good is built of mental blocks, cemented together by fear and unbelief, mixed in the mortar of negative experience. It is not necessary that impoverishment and pain accompany you in your experience through life.

SAY:

I know that there is a Presence, a Power and a Law within me, irresistibly drawing everything into my experience which makes life worthwhile.

I know that friendship, love and riches, health, harmony and happiness are mine.

I know that nothing but good can go out from me, therefore the good that I receive is but the completion of a circle—the fulfillment of my desire for all.

I refuse to judge according to appearances, either mental or physical, no matter what the thought says, or what the appearance seems to be.

There is always a higher Power.

Upon this Power I rely with absolute confidence that It will never fail me.

I repudiate all evil, cast out every fear that accompanied it, and continuously exercise the dominion which rightfully belongs to me.

Discover Your
Inner Perfection

It is only as you live affirmatively that you can be happy. Knowing that there is but one Spirit in which everyone lives, moves, and has his or her being, you are to feel this Spirit not only in your consciousness but also in your affairs. You are united with all. You are one with the eternal Light Itself. The Presence of Spirit within you blesses everyone you meet, tends to heal everything you touch, brings gladness into the life of everyone you contact. Therefore, you are a blessing to yourself, to humankind and to the day in which you live.

SAY:

Today I uncover the perfection within me. In its fullness I reveal the indwelling Kingdom. I look out upon the world of my affairs, knowing that the Spirit within me makes my way both correct and easy.

I know there is nothing in me that could possibly obstruct or withhold the Divine circuit of Life and Love, which God is.

My word dissolves every negative thought or impulse that could throw a shadow over my perfection.

Wisdom shines through my thoughts and actions.

Life harmonizes my body so that it is revitalized and manifests perfection in every cell, organ and function.

Love harmonizes my mind so that joy sings in my heart.

I am in complete unity with Good.

Security Is Yours Right Now

Do not be like Job, who exclaimed: ". . . the thing which I greatly feared is come upon me. . . ." Instead, release your fears and know that the Mind of God guides you in everything you do and makes the path ahead of you one of joy, happiness and security. Your life is always in the hands of God, and if you permit, you will be led in ways that protect you and safely carry you through every experience.

SAY:

I know that Divine Intelligence now helps me control my thinking and causes me to expect only good things to come into my experience.

As I now accept Its guidance, It flows through me and out into everything I do and into every situation.

I know that today and every day the Power of the Living Spirit makes perfect the way before me.

Divine Intelligence is always acting upon my mind, telling me what is best to do, counseling me wisely, and guiding me gently but surely into pathways of prosperity, happiness and physical health.

I am ever protected by the Love of God; I am secure in the hands of God.

Every sense of anxiety and insecurity is now dissolved and fades away.

Only good comes to me and goes out from me.

This is what I expect.

This is what I accept as my experience.

How to Experience Inspiration

The disciple John tells us that Jesus said, "God is a Spirit: and they that worship him must worship him in spirit and in truth." Wonderful indeed is the conception of the union of all life, which Jesus proclaimed in the ecstasy of his illumination: "I and my Father are one." All cause and all effect proceed from the invisible Spirit. You are one with this Spirit and cannot be separated from It. Your word has power because your word is the action of God through your thought.

SAY:

I now clarify my vision and purify my thought, so that it becomes a mirror reflecting inspiration directly from the secret place of the Most High at the center of my own being.

I do this by quiet contemplation; not through strenuous effort but by learning to *fast* to all negation and to *feast* upon the affirmations of spiritual realization.

I know that I need never break before the onslaught of any confusion that exists around me.

Today I walk in the light of God's Love.

I am guided and my guidance is multiplied.

There is an inspiration within me which governs every act and every thought . . . in certainty, with conviction and in peace.

I know that the key which unlocks the treasure-house, the key to the kingdom of God, is in my spiritual hand, and I enter in and experience that kingdom today.

This is the kingdom of God's creation.

How to Save
Yourself Trouble

It is impossible for you to experience the full joy of living while you iden-tify yourself with anything less than that. The images of your thought attract to you, and you are attracted to . . . people, circumstances and situations which are like them. Once you fully realize this you will understand that to change undesirable conditions, or to protect yourself from them, you must of necessity change the basic pattern of your thought.

This requires that you must constantly be on guard as to what you allow to enter your mind, or to arise from negative memories of the past. When such thoughts are in any way contrary to your greatest good they must be immedi-ately discarded and replaced with their opposites, those ideas affirming only your welfare in every respect.

SAY:

I know that I am a child of the Most High.

I am one with the Intelligence and Perfection that is back of everything.

As it is the nature of thought to externalize itself, bringing about conditions which exactly correspond to the thought, I affirm that my thoughts are Divinely guided.

I entertain only constructive ideas; all others I willingly discard.

I am aware that there is a Principle of Perfection at the center of my being, an invisible Presence that forever externalizes Itself for me and through me in every avenue of life, today and every day.

Eliminate Negative Situations from Your Life

Good is at the root of everything, regardless of its seeming absence. But this good must be recognized. Since there is but one Spirit and this Spirit is in you and in everything, then everywhere you go you will meet this Spirit. You meet this Spirit in people, in places and in things. This one Spirit, which manifests Itself in and through all, including yourself, automatically adjusts parts to the whole.

Therefore, you may accept with positive certainty that the Spirit within you does go before you and prepares your way. Your faith is placed in something positive, certain as the laws of life, exact as the principles of mathematics. It is the vital, living Force that supports all of your thoughts and deeds when they are in harmony with It.

SAY:

I know that the Spirit within me goes before me, making perfect, plain, straight, easy and happy the pathway of my experience.

There is nothing in me that can obstruct the Divine circuits of Life, of Wholeness and Perfection.

My affirmative word dissolves every negative thought or impulse that would throw a shadow of imperfection across the threshold of my experience.

I identify myself only with the Living Spirit—with all the Power, all the Presence and all the Life there is.

I lift my cup of acceptance, knowing that the Divine outpouring will fill it to the brim.

How to Insure That the Right Things Happen

Right action means that every legitimate and constructive purpose you have in mind shall be successfully executed. It means that you will know what to do, how to think, how to act, how to proceed. You definitely know that if your thought is in accord with the Divine Nature, it actually is the Law of God enforcing Itself in your experience. Hence, there is nothing in you or around you that can limit your constructive thought. The Power of this Law is within you and the action which results from this Power produces harmony, peace, joy and success.

SAY:

I know that in this consciousness of the Divine Nature is the supply for my every need—physical, mental or spiritual— and I accept that supply in deepest gratitude.

I am thankful that this is the way Life fulfills my needs, through the doorway of my inner self, and I am thankful that I know how to use this perfect Law.

I come to this great Fountain of Supply in the very center of my being to absorb that for which I have need, mentally and physically; and I am filled with the sense of the reality of that which I desire.

I permit this awareness to flow into my world of thought and action, knowing that it brings peace, harmony and order all around me.

There arises within me renewed faith in the limitless resources of the Divine Presence, the perfect Law, and there is now right action in all my ways.

Free Yourself from Fear Today

To have your heart be without fear is to have implicit confidence in the good, the enduring and the true. Fear is the only thing of which to be afraid. It is not the host encamped against you, nor the confusion around you that you need to fear; it is lack of confidence in the good alone which should concern you. Through inner spiritual vision you know that good alone is permanent and all else is transitory. You know that right finally dissolves everything opposed to it. The power of Spirit is supreme over every antagonist. Therefore, you should cherish no fear, and when you neither fear nor hate you come to understand the unity of Life.

SAY:

I realize that fear is not Godlike, since it contradicts the Divine Presence, repudiates limitless Love, and denies infinite Good.

Fear is neither person, place nor thing; it is merely an impostor that I have believed in; I have entertained it so long that it seems as if it really were something.

Today I repudiate all fear.

I renounce all thoughts of hate.

I enter into conscious union with the Spirit.

I accept Good as supreme, positive and absolute.

With joy I enter into the activities of the day; without regret I remember the events of yesterday; and with confidence I look forward to tomorrow, for today my heart is without fear.

Release Your Invisible Spiritual Power

Everything in nature is an individualization of one coordinating Life—one Presence and one Law of being. Our minds have become so filled with things which contradict this that even the Truth has to await our recognition. We must learn to become consciously aware of the Divine Presence and the Divine Power; the wholeness of Truth, of Love and of Reason. Instead of dwelling on negative thoughts, let us dwell on peace and joy, discover the power of he invisible Spirit working in and through us now, and lay hold of this realization with complete certainty.

SAY:

I know that I am a perfect being now, living under perfect conditions today.

Knowing that Spirit alone is real, I know there is one Power which acts and reacts in my experience, in my body, and in my thought, for my good.

I know that this recognition establishes, through Law, harmony in my experience, prosperity, a sense of happiness, peace, health and joy.

Today I hold communion with this invisible Presence which peoples the world with the manifestations of Its life, Its light and Its love.

I withdraw the veil which hides my real self and draw close to the Spirit within, that is in everything and in everyone.

I accept everything that belongs to this Spirit.

I claim everything that partakes of Its nature.

Express Your Inner Perfection

When you go up onto a mountain in your consciousness and lift your thought above the confusion of everything that seems to be disconnected and dissociated, you become unified with the pattern of spiritual Cause back of all things. In psychosomatic medicine, and in all psychological adjustment, the suggestion of a universal pattern back of things, a pattern which in itself and of itself must be perfect, is automatically being dealt with. Affirming the perfection of God in all things, manifesting in and through each and every thing in a unique way, is no idle statement.

SAY:

I affirm the perfection of the Divine Pattern at the center of my being.

Realizing Its reality, I permit Its essence to flow through me, claiming it as my very own.

Believing in Its wholeness, perfection and right action, I know that everything in my experience conforms to Its nature.

Accepting Its peace, I am calm.

Expressing Its love, I am unified with life.

Believing in Its power, with childlike faith I accept the authority of Its action in my everyday affairs.

Today I declare the presence and activity of Spirit in that which I am, in my relationships with others, and in my contacts with the world about me.

How to Find
Solutions

God is the Presence and the Power that knows all things and can do all things. And if you will but take your personal problem to that high summit of your own consciousness and feel that the answer takes the place of the problem, then the problem will be solved. You need to know there is nothing in you that can keep this from happening; there is no doubt or limitation in your mind. You should feel that the answer is established in your consciousness and is known to you, right now, in your present experience. To find the solution to a problem, let go of the problem, and definitely expect the answer.

SAY:

I know that my every thought and act is governed by a superior Intelligence.

There is *something* in me that knows what to do.

It not only knows what to do, but It compels me to act upon what It knows.

Therefore, everything I ought to do, I shall do; anything I ought to know, I shall know.

Whatever seeming problems or difficulties may confront me, with complete assurance I accept Divine guidance.

Right now there is the right solution for my every problem.

There is an inner, quiet, flowing stream of Life that carries me surely and safely to my proper destination and to the accomplishment of my every good purpose.

Attaining a
High Consciousness

When Jesus spoke of being "lifted up from the earth," he meant that what is human about you must consciously become united with the Divine. In ancient writings, the earth stood for the lowest form of life, while heaven represented the highest. Therefore, being lifted up from the earth means uniting with heaven. This daily lifting up of your thought is necessary if you wish to unite yourself and everything you are doing with the Divine, so spiritual Power flows through you and into all your acts.

SAY:

I now turn to the Spirit within me.

I know that It is close to me, It is what I am, and It governs my life in harmony and in peace.

I know that through me, It brings joy and happiness to everyone I meet.

Through the Power of this indwelling Spirit I am a blessing to myself and others.

I lift up my whole mind to the realization that the Spirit of God is within me and that this perfect Spirit is my *real* self.

I invite the Spirit to direct my thoughts and acts, and I accept that It is now doing so.

I expect new ideas to stimulate my imagination and direct me into new ways of doing things.

I expect new circumstances and situations.

The action of Divine Intelligence within me impels me to act for the greatest benefit of myself and others.

Nonresistance: The Key to Real Victory

Gandhi built his whole philosophy of life around the theory of nonviolence. An ancient Chinese sage said that all things are possible to him who can perfectly practice inaction. Jesus said to "resist not evil." Surely some truth must be contained in these simple thoughts. If so—if there is a spiritual transcendence of consciousness which dissolves problems—then you ought to learn about it and use it.

Think of an iceberg, with the sun's rays falling on it. Soon it will dissolve. That which was an obstruction becomes liquid. Perhaps that is the meaning of spiritual transcendence, inner awareness and the power of nonviolence. The great, the good and the wise have known this, and you can know it, too.

SAY:

Today I practice nonresistance.

Disregarding everything that seems to contradict the Reality in which I believe, I affirm that Reality is operating in my life.

Turning resolutely from everything that denies the good I wish to experience, I affirm that good.

In the midst of fear, I proclaim faith.

At the center of uncertainty, I proclaim security.

In the midst of want, I proclaim abundance.

Where unhappiness seems to exist, I announce joy.

There is no situation or condition that resists these transcendent thoughts, for they proclaim the omnipotence of God and the Divine guidance of the Mind that can accomplish all things.

How to Attract
Good Things

You are either attracting or repelling, according to your mental attitudes. You are either identifying yourself with lack or with abundance, with love and friendship or with indifference. You cannot keep from attracting into your experience that which corresponds to the sum total of your states of consciousness. This law of attraction and repulsion works automatically. It is like the law of reflection—the reflection corresponds to the object held before a mirror.

How careful, then, you should be to guard your thoughts, not only seeing to it that you keep them free from doubt and fear—accepting only the good—but, equally, consciously repelling every thought which denies that good.

SAY:

I know that accepting only good in my life penetrates any unbelief in my mind, casts out fear, removes doubt and clears away obstacles, permitting that which is enduring, perfect and true to be realized.

I have complete faith and acceptance that all the worthwhile ideas I now affirm will be fulfilled as I have believed.

I do everything with a sense of reliance upon the Law of Mind, therefore I know that my word shall not return unto me void.

I accept this word and rejoice in it.

I expect complete and successful fulfillment of the thoughts of increased good which I now establish.

Straighten Out Your Life

Through affirmative thinking you are able to clear your mind of negative thoughts, fears and doubts. You must do this if you are to become aware of the Presence, Peace and Harmony of God that is within and around you. All the good you desire awaits your acceptance of it, but you cannot experience it while you deny it. The key to right thinking and right living is the steady affirmative pattern of belief that only God's Good enters your life.

SAY:

God is all Power, all Presence and all Peace.

I now let go of all fear, doubt and confusion, and turn my thought and attention to the belief that only good is my experience.

I have faith enough to believe that God is Perfect, and that nothing unlike that Perfection could be His desire for creation.

Peace and happiness, joy and contentment always walk with me.

I am surrounded by Divine right action, and It flows through my every experience.

I patiently brush aside every doubt or fear that enters my mind and resolutely accept only the wonderful things of the kingdom of God, here and now.

God is all the Power there is, all the Presence there is, and all the Life there is, and only that which is of the nature of God enters my life.

Connecting with Inner Joy

You are part of the universal Mind, one with the universal Substance. You live, move and have your being in pure Spirit. All the abundance, the power and the harmony of this Spirit exists at the center of your being. You experience this good in such degree as you accept, believe in and feel it. As you enter into life, feeling the Divine Presence in everything, more and more you will hear a Song of Joy singing at the center of your being. You have only to be still and listen to this Song of Life, for It is always there.

SAY:

Knowing the Divine Presence is always closer to me than my very breath, I have nothing to fear.

I feel this loving protection around me.

I know that the Song of Joy, of Love and of Peace, is forever chanting Its hymn of praise and beauty at the center of my being; therefore I tune out of my mind all unhappy and negative ideas.

I direct my thought to the sunshine of life, to brightness and laughter, to the joyous presence of radiant Spirit.

I lay aside all anxiety, all striving, and I let Divine Love operate through me into my affairs.

Joyfully I anticipate greater abundance, more success and a deeper peace.

Joy wells up within my mind, and Life sings Its song of ecstasy in my heart.

The Spiritual Approach to Making Money

Spirit fills all space and animates every form, therefore Spirit is the true actor in everything. But Spirit can only act for you by acting through you. This means simply that God can only give you what you take. As you daily enter into your Divine inheritance, with your thought and heart, you enter into the realm of absolute Causation. Completely believe that from this secret place of the Most High within you an objective manifestation of your every legitimate desire is projected. Are you really accepting abundance? Is your thought really animating your experience with the idea of plenty? Are you affirming that Divine Substance is forever flowing to you as supply?

SAY:

Today I praise the abundance of all things.

I animate everything with the idea of abundance.

I am remembering only the good; I am expecting more good; I am experiencing good.

I acknowledge that the Spirit is working everywhere.

I give thanks that the right action of Spirit is flowing into my experience in ever-increasing volume.

There is *that* within me which sees, knows and understands this truth, which completely accepts it.

There is good enough to go around.

Therefore I do not withhold that good from myself or others, but constantly proclaim spiritual abundance is forever flowing to each and all as supply.

I now accept as mine all that is needed to make my life a joyous experience.

Personal Peace . . . World Peace

A basic Harmony must exist at the center of everything or the Universe Itself would be a chaos. You already know this and believe it; now you are going to act upon it. You are not only going to believe in it, you are going to act as though it were true, because it is true. There is peace at the center of your being—a peace that can be felt through the day and in the cool of the evening when you have turned from your labor and the first star shines in the soft light of the sky. It broods over the earth quietly, tenderly, as a mother watches over her child.

SAY:

In this peace that holds me so gently I find strength and protection from all fear or anxiety.

It is the peace of God, in which I feel the love of a Holy Presence.

I am so conscious of this love, this protection, that every sense of fear slips away from me as mist fades in the morning light.

I see good in everything, God personified in all people, Life manifest in every event.

Spirit is not separate from persons or events; I see that It unites everything with Itself, vitalizing all with the energy of Its own being, creating everything through Its own Divine imagination, surrounding everything with peace and quiet and calm.

I am one with this deep, abiding peace.

I know that all is well.

Accept Only Good

The good in which you believe can triumph over every evil you have experienced. You have a silent partnership with the Infinite. This partnership has never been dissolved; it never can be. You are to have implicit confidence in your own ability, knowing that it is the nature of thought to externalize itself in your health and affairs, knowing that you are the thinker. You are going to turn resolutely from every sense of lack, want and limitation, and declare that the perfect Law of God is operating in, for and through you.

SAY:

I have complete confidence in my knowledge and understanding of the Law of Mind.

I not only know what the Law is, I know how to use It.

I know that I shall obtain definite results through the use of It.

Knowing this, having confidence in my ability to use the Law and using It daily for specific purposes, gradually I build up an unshakable faith, both in the Law and the possibility of demonstrating It.

Therefore, today I declare that my thoughts shall only be affirmative, positive and constructive.

Today I believe that "underneath are the everlasting arms," and I rest in this Divine assurance and this Divine security.

I know that not only is all well with my mind and my body—but all is also well with my affairs.

Having a Healthy Body

Your body, every part of it, is a manifestation of Spirit. Its perfect pattern in the Mind of God cannot deteriorate. This instant, the Divine vitality that constantly flows through you takes form in the likeness of perfect, whole, complete cells. Every cell of your body is strong and healthy, filled with life, vitality and strength. Your body, Spirit in form, knows no time, knows no degree; it knows only to express fully, instantaneously.

SAY:

I recognize that Spirit is within me and It is that which I am.

I let this recognition of my indwelling Divinity flow through my entire consciousness.

I let it reach down into the very depths of my being.

I rejoice in my Divinity.

I am now made vigorous, robust and mentally creative.

I am fortified with God's perfection and right action.

I am healthy and able-bodied.

The Life of God is my life.

The Strength of God is my strength.

The Mind of God is my mind.

Every breath I draw fills me with perfection; it vitalizes, upbuilds and renews every cell of my body.

I am born *in* Spirit and *of* Spirit, and I am Spirit made manifest this instant.

Spirit Is Already Within You

The Spirit of God is an undivided and indivisible Wholeness. It fills all time with Its presence and permeates space with the activity of Its thought. Your endeavor, then, is not so much to find God as it is to realize His Presence and to understand that this Presence is always with you. Nothing can be nearer to you than that which is the very essence of your being. Your outward search for God culminates in the greatest of all possible discoveries—finding Him at the center of your own being. Life flows up from within you.

SAY:

I know that my search is over.

I am consciously aware of the Presence of the Spirit.

I have discovered the great Reality.

I am awake to the realization of this Presence.

There is but One Life.

Today I see It reflected in every form, back of every countenance, moving through every act.

I know that the Divine Presence is everywhere.

I salute the good in everything.

I recognize God-Life responding to me in every person I meet, in every event that transpires, in every circumstance in my experience.

I feel the warmth and color of this Divine Presence forevermore pressing against me, forevermore welling up from within me—the wellspring of Eternal Being, present yesterday, today, tomorrow and always.

Claim Your Wholeness

Regardless of what negative condition may exist in your physical body, in the Mind of God there is a pattern of perfection for your body. Otherwise it never could have been created to begin with, or sustained and renewed. Your life is of God. Your health is the expression of the Perfection of Spirit within you. As you recognize that there is a River of Life within you which flows from the eternal Source of all Life, you need to open your mind and accept the full influx of Its life-giving Power.

SAY:

I now affirm that every organ, action and function of my physical body is animated by the living Spirit.

There is one perfect Mind directing my thoughts, one complete Wholeness sustaining my being, one Divine circulation flowing through me.

By day and by night I realize that the Divine Life flowing through me is renewing every cell of my body after the image of Its own perfection. I give thanks for this silent Power which sustains me, and I say to my own mind: "You are to believe in this Power. You are to accept It. You are to let It flow through you, for you are one with It. There is no other power, no other presence and no other life; therefore, all the Power there is, all the Presence there is, and all the Life there is, is sustaining you now and will continue to sustain you."

Using the Mental Power Within You

It is possible that you have been using the power of your mind to produce the very limitation from which you wish to extricate yourself. Realizing that in your ignorance you may have been doing this, you need not condemn yourself or anyone else. Aware of the fact that you are a child of God, as are all people, you need to express your Divine heritage. As your thinking is patterned after your highest concept of spiritual Perfection, so will your life reflect such thoughts.

SAY:

Today, realizing that my life is truly a reflection of what I think, I now permit the Spirit within me to guide and direct my thoughts and emotions.

The Divine influx refreshes me daily, and I feel myself saturated with the Life Essence Itself; I feel It flowing in and through me.

I now know myself to be a perfect instrument in Life's Divine Symphony, in tune with Its Harmony and Perfection.

My body is an instrument in, through and upon which Life plays a Divine and Perfect Harmony.

I do not search for other powers, for there is only One Power, the Power which I am going to use, the Power which I already know possesses eternity and is already at the center of my own life.

I know that this Power does now heal every negative circumstance, overcome every obstacle and free me from every false condition. And so it is.

Getting Free of Bad Influences

The kingdom of God is at hand. The riches, power, glory and might of this kingdom are yours today. You do not rob others by entering into the fullness of your kingdom of joy, your kingdom of abundance. But you must recognize that all people belong to the same kingdom. You merely claim for yourself what you would like the Divine Spirit to do unto all.

The eternal is forever filled with the Presence of perfect Life. You always have been, and forever will remain, a complete and perfect expression of the eternal Mind which is God, the living Spirit Almighty. You are a creation of Spirit and have Divine heritage.

SAY:

Today I enter into the limitless variations of self-expression which the Divine Spirit projects into my experience.

Knowing that all experience is a play of Life upon Itself, Love blossoming into self-expression, Good coming forth into the joy of Its own being, I enter into the game of living with joyful anticipation, with enthusiasm.

Today I enter into my Divine inheritance, freeing my thought from the belief that undesirable external conditions imposed upon me are necessary and unchangeable.

I declare the freedom of my Divine sonship, and imbibe of the fullness Life has to offer.

Healing What Needs to Be Healed

You need to develop an understanding that although your body is real and tangible, with definite form and outline, it is at the same time somehow made of a living "stuff" which is saturated with God-Life. Whatever the stuff is of which your body is made, though it is called material, it must really be made of the Essence of which all things are made. Therefore, you need to sense within the very cells and tissues of your body, an Eternality.

SAY:

Realizing that the Spirit within me is God, being fully conscious of this Divine Presence as the sustaining Principle of my life, I open my thought to Its influx.

I open my consciousness to Its outpouring, carrying with It all the power of the Infinite.

I know that silently I am drawing into my experience today and every day an ever-increasing measure of vitality, health, joy and harmony.

Divinely guided, everything I think, say and do is quickened into right action, into productive action, into increased action.

My invisible perfect pattern already exists.

My faith, drawing upon this source, causes that which was unseen to become visible.

The harmonious action of Life now permeates every part of my being and experience.

All the good that exists is mine *now*.

Physical Perfection
Is Yours Now!

Your body is a temple of the living Spirit. It is spiritual substance. Since the Spirit of God has entered into your being, your life is spiritual. The supreme Being, ever present, exists at the very center of your thought. This Presence within you has the power to make all things new.

SAY:

I know that the perfect Life of God is in and through me, in every part of my being.

As the sun dissolves the mist, so my acceptance of Life dissolves all pain and discord.

It remolds and re-creates my body after the likeness of the Divine pattern which exists in the Mind of God.

Even now the living Spirit is flowing through me. I open wide the doorway of my consciousness to Its influx.

I permit my physical body to receive the flow of Spirit in every action, function, cell and organ. I know that my whole being manifests the life, love, peace, harmony, strength and joy of the Spirit which indwells me, which is incarnated in me, which is my entire being.

I realize that all the Power and Presence there is clothes me in Its eternal embrace; that the Spirit forever imparts its Life to me.

I know that the Spirit within me is my strength and power.

Why Be Incomplete in a Complete Universe?

You are some part of the Divine Whole, and the Power and the Presence of the Spirit is in the word you speak, and that word instantly and perfectly and permanently makes things whole. Know that you are an individualization of the Spirit—which is the Source of wholeness, love, reason and intelligence. Empty yourself of any and every thought that denies this. Know, silently but effectively, that the Divine Power of the invisible Spirit works in you here and now.

SAY:

I take hold of this realization with complete certainty.

I recognize that I am a perfect being, living under perfect conditions, knowing that Spirit alone is real.

I also know that Mind alone is the only thing that has any power either to act or to react.

Everything I think, say or do today shall be thought, said or done from the spiritual viewpoint of God in everything.

My recognition of this Power is sufficient to neutralize every false experience, making the crooked straight and the rough places smooth.

I definitely know that this recognition establishes harmony in my experience as well as prosperity and a sense of happiness and health.

As I now discard and release all ideas to the contrary, I experience complete wholeness.

The Secret to Good Physical Health

There is an eternal newness of Life. You are one with Life, and the Spirit is continually creating in and through you. There is no darkness, despair or discouragement in the Mind that creates all. But we humans have sought out many devious ways to deprive ourselves of the abundant Good that is always available to us. Your mind and thought contain the key to successful living. You are the captain of your soul.

SAY:

I have the will to be well, to be happy and to live in joy.

I affirm that there is only the likeness of good health in my experience.

I am seeing this good, believing in it, thinking about it and expecting it to continue.

All that I do, I do with joy.

All whom I meet, I embrace with thoughts of love.

Realizing that I am rooted in pure Spirit, I trace my life and being back to its original Source, and I know that every activity of my physical body is now in perfect rhythm with the One Perfect Life.

All my ideas to the contrary are discarded, eliminated. In their place there is established the complete conviction that my body is the temple of the living God.

I am made new and whole in this moment as the Love of God permeates me.

God's Life is my life now!

Adding New Meaning to Life

It is impossible for you to receive that which your mind refuses to accept. If you desire to receive more, you need to consciously develop the ability to mentally encompass it. You make your life mean and little, limiting its possibilities when you refuse to accept the whole gift of God. As you open your consciousness to a greater receptivity of the Divine, to an enlarged concept of the good that can flood your experience, life will take on a new and wonderful meaning.

SAY:

I now tell myself that my thoughts are filled only with greater anticipation of a fuller life.

My thinking now expands, and I know that a greater good than anything I have ever conceived is coming into my experience.

Without reservation I believe this and accept it as being so.

My mind and body are continuously open to the Divine influx of all that makes for vital, joyous living.

The quiet but sure right action of God peacefully readjusts everything in my life as I surrender all ignorance, doubt and fear.

As I now cleanse my mind of thoughts contrary to my greater good and come to dwell only on those ideas which create health, wholeness and happiness, the abundance of God's kingdom fills every moment of all my days.

Don't Let Anything Get in Your Way

Everything in the universe is a unique individualization or expression of the One Thing, which is the Cause of all things. You should become aware that the one creative Power is expressing in you in a unique way and that It is always pressing against you seeking a fuller outlet of Its infinite possibilities. You do not have to imitate or compete, for you are a special creation of God, as is everyone else, and you have full access to the unlimited potential of infinite Intelligence.

SAY:

Today I practice being myself, and seek to reveal more fully the miracle of Life. I discover a fuller delight in living, and in the wonder of Being that continually wells up within me.

I think simply and directly from the center of my being, which is God, the living Spirit.

I enter into the faith of believing, the joy of knowing and the act of living—which proclaim the one Power and the one Presence in all things.

Today, as a child would, I accept this Presence that responds to me in a personal, warm and colorful way. It fills me with vitality, opens my mind to greater vistas, and imbues me with a love for all life.

As I now accept my partnership with the Infinite I discover a new freedom.

My thoughts soar, my experiences expand and unbounded joy fills my being.

Dealing with Fear of Death

Life has set the stamp of individuality on you. You are different from any other person who ever lived. You are an individualized center in the Consciousness of God. You are an individualized activity in the Action of God. You are you, and you are eternal. Therefore, do not wait for immortality. The resurrection of life is today. Begin to live today as though you are an immortal being and all thought of death, all fear of change, will slip from you. You will step out of the tomb of uncertainty into the light of eternal day.

SAY:

I know that every apparent death is a resurrection; therefore, gladly I die to everything that is unlike the good of God.

Silently I pass from less to more, from isolation into inclusion, from separation into oneness.

Today, realizing that there is nothing in my past which can rise against me, nothing in my future which can menace the unfoldment of my experience, I know life shall be an eternal adventure.

I revel in the contemplation of the immeasurable future, the path of eternal progress, the everlastingness of my own being, the ongoing of my soul, the daily renewed energy and action of Divinity within me which has forever set the stamp of individualized Being on my mind.

Universal Power Is Yours to Use

The all-intelligent, creative Presence is the source of all that you are. You need to believe in the ability and the willingness of this great Source to sustain Its own creation. The Kingdom and the Power and the Glory of God express through you. Recognize yourself to be a center through which the Intelligence and Power of the universe find expression. Infinite Mind, operating through you, can bring to you the manifestation of harmony, order and the highest good. Through It, the consciousness of peace and plenty is established within you. All that is necessary to your happiness and well-being belongs in your experience.

SAY:

There can be neither limitation nor lack in my life, for nothing has happened to the one perfect Activity.

As It now freely flows through me, I am freed from any sense of bondage.

All power is given unto me from on High.

Knowing this, I am strong with the strength of the all-vitalizing Power of the universe.

I am sustained and inspired by a Divine stream of Spirit-Energy which flows through me as enthusiasm and vital ideas.

Every aspect of my mind responds to this spiritual flow.

Creativity and inspiration are my Divine birthright and I now express them to the fullest.

How to Accomplish Worthwhile Things

If you surrender your whole being to the Divine Spirit, knowing that of your own human self you can do nothing, you get rid of that self which is impotent. You brush aside its weakness, its fears, its doubts, its misunderstandings and its uncertainties, and you think back to that Divine center within you which is God.

Come to believe in the power and presence of the Spirit within you. Accept Its power and permit Its guidance. Feel that you are speaking from this center of Divine certainty within you when you state: "There is One Life, that Life is God, that Life is my Life now."

SAY:

I know there is a Presence of Perfection at the center of my being.

I feel the Divine Life flowing through me, animating every atom of my being.

And I feel that everyone else is of like nature—we all live and move and have our being in God.

I now affirm with complete acceptance that the Intelligence which created all things is leading and guiding me into the accomplishment of every good and worthwhile purpose.

This Presence exists at the very center of my being and is flowing through me, establishing happiness, joy, abundance, harmonious living and a constructive use of the creative power of my mind. I am now open to new ideas, new hopes and new aspirations.

The Secret of
Joyous Living

You need to awake to a new joy of living. Whatever there may have been of fear, doubt or uncertainty in the past, realize that today is a new beginning. Your world can be made new from this moment.

Have the will to be well, to be happy and to live in joy. Recognize that nothing in your past can deny you the privilege of living happily, and nothing in the future can bring anything other than joy to you. Learn to find only good in your daily experience. As you discover your daily good and believe in it and think about it, you will expect it to continue.

SAY:

Realizing that I am rooted in pure Spirit, I trace my life back to its original Source and find that every activity of my mind and body is in rhythm with the one perfect Life.

This Life circulates through me now, eliminating anything that does not belong.

It now makes perfect every action of assimilation, circulation and elimination in my body.

Having the will to live in joy and in wholeness, I am at peace with the world about me.

My desire is to live and to let live, to give and to forgive, and to see in every person I meet the Divine likeness.

As I now release every sense of depression or limitation, I am lifted up into a new joy of living by the Giver of all Life.

My heart sings a song of happiness and freedom.

Establishing
Peace of Mind

The Divine Presence is already what you are, and It contains the possibility of all joy in living. You should not entertain any thought that would limit your experience of the good life. Nothing in you can separate you from the Divine Presence, though in many ways you are able to inhibit Its flow through you. But the greater possibility of knowing the Love of God, increased joy of living and greater good in life is yours for the accepting.

SAY:

I affirm that the Spirit within me is evermore leading me on the pathway of joyful living.

It is forever directing my thoughts, my words and my actions into constructive channels of self-expression.

It is forever uniting me with others in love, kindliness and consideration.

I live and move and have my being in the infinite sea of perfect Life, in the Divine Presence from which I cannot become separated.

I accept the Divine Presence as the great Reality.

I know that the kingdom of God is within me.

I have complete trust that the Law of Mind will make manifest in my experience my every good desire.

Everything necessary to my happiness is now established in Mind and does become an established fact in my experience.

Find Peace by Letting Go of Problems

As you learn to give all of your burdens to the right action of God, you will find that everything falls into its proper place. You let your problems slip away from you, realizing that a Power greater than you are and a Presence that is within you is ready, willing and able to guide you in all ways. Then peace, security and fulfillment come with ease, and there is a sense of joy and accomplishment.

SAY:

I now release all thoughts of fear, doubt and uncertainty, knowing that the infinite Intelligence of the Spirit within me knows what to do and how to do it, and does it with ease.

This Intelligence guides my every thought and act.

Everything I do shall be a joy and shall prosper.

My every encounter with others shall be a blessing for all.

The right action that manifests in my life also works for all others.

Loving, I know that I am loved.

Giving, I know that Life shall give back to me.

Reaching within me to that which is Divine, I now invite the Presence of God to make Itself known through me, bringing joy and happiness into my life and the lives of those about me.

Resting in calm faith and quiet expectancy, I know there shall be only happiness and joy in every situation in which I find myself.

Greater Possibilities
Are Yours Now!

There is always a greater possibility available to you. There is a Divine Strength and an infinite Wisdom at the center of your being, ever waiting to be released. It will enable you to put more into life and living and to take more out, also. A limitless Creativity expresses through all that is, and It is always seeking a fuller channel of expression through you. Recognize that It exists, and accept Its action in your life.

SAY:

I now lift up my whole thought to the inflow of Divine Strength and infinite Wisdom.

I know that I am in a silent partnership with God—today, tomorrow and every day.

I accept the creative action and direction of the Spirit within me.

I know that new doorways are opened, that new opportunities for self-expression are now presenting themselves.

New ideas are coming into my mind.

I am meeting new situations.

I expect to accomplish and achieve.

Divine Intelligence flows through me, inspiring me, directing me into ever more worthwhile goals of creative endeavor.

God guides me in every way and new horizons of joyous living continually open up before me.

I accept the fullness of Life this moment.

How to
Find Harmony

You live in the house of God, as do all other people. The house of God is filled with people of Divine origin, whose divinity will be revealed to you if you allow it to be. As you look at the divinity in them, they tend to see the divinity in you, for this is the way of life. Everyone responds to you at the level of your recognition of them.

In the household of God there is no jealousy, no littleness or meanness. It is a household of joy, a place of happiness and contentment. There is warmth, color and beauty. Seen in this light, your negative earthly experiences and associations are largely what you have made them, rather than being what they might have been if you had allowed God to manage things.

SAY:

I know that in the house of experience in which I live, the host is God and all people are guests.

The invitation has been eternally written for all to enter and dwell therein as the guests of this eternal Host, in joy, integrity and friendship.

I do now fully accept my Divine obligation to express only love and appreciation to and for everyone I encounter, knowing that what I think, say and do returns to me.

I permit Divine Love to operate through me into my daily concerns.

Now only harmonious, happy and mutually beneficial relationships fill my life.

I rejoice in the Divine Harmony which surrounds me.

Unity with All Life

You live because Life lives in you. You move because a universal Energy flows through you. You think because an infinite Intelligence thinks through you. You exist because the Divine Spirit seeks to individualize Itself in and as you. This is why you are called the temple of the Living God. There is a Divine spark at the center of your being. But you need to recognize this, believe it and act upon your belief.

SAY:

I now recognize my Divine birthright.

I consciously enter into my partnership with God in joy, love and a sense of peace.

I know that I live, move and have my being in the Life of the Spirit.

God seeks to express through me in a little different form than anyone else.

I now accept my responsibility to be what I truly am and to live up to all that Life seeks to be through me.

There is a place in my mind that merges with the Mind of God, and I now draw power and inspiration from it.

The radiance of the Presence of God envelops me.

In this knowledge of Unity with God, everything in my life is constructive, life-giving, blessed and prospered.

I joyously express the Nature of God.

INDEX

A

Absolute Intelligence, 214
acceptance, 80–81
Active Principle, 172
Activity of Mind, 28
affirmations
    for abundance, 224
    for happiness, 223
    for love, 225
    for problems, 224
    for right action, 223
    for security, 224–25
    for success, 224
Alexander, Franz, 20
Apocrypha, 203
    on God, 135
    on Unity of God, 164
applied religion, 214
Atma-Buddhi, 172–73
Atman, 172
atmosphere of body, 18
Augustine, on temple of God, 167
awakening, process of, 164–65
Awakening of Faith, 163

B

balance, 179–80
Beauty, 44
believing, 9–10

Bhagavad-Gita, 202
Bible
    on awakening to union
        with God, 173
    on balance, 180
    on creation, 139–40
    on God, 134
    as guide to eternal values, 113
    on healing with faith, 183–84
    on immortality, 150
    on separation from source, 145
    on Spirit Incarnate, 144
    on spirit and mind, 177–78
    stress on prosperity through
        spiritualizing the mind, 189
    on Unity of God, 162, 163
Blanton, Smiley, 63
bodies, as manifestations of the
    Supreme Spirit, 181
Book of the Dead, 180, 202
breath of God, 175–76
Brierley, J., 174
British Medical Journal, 20
Browning, Robert, 156, 160, 213
Buddha, 124, 180, 202
Buddhism, 135

C

Causation, 141

309

healing *(continued)*
   as clearing the consciousness
     of discord, 182
   in other traditions, 184
healing arts, inevitable progress
   in, 187
health
   achieving by thinking, 15–24
   available through right
     thinking, 15
   choice of, 22–23
   effect of personality on, 69
   meditation on, 102–3
   response to emotional status,
     92–93
   using creative ability for, 101
Health, Disease and Integration,
   55
Hebrews, 141
Heisenberg, 217n 2
helpful traits, 48–49
Hermes Trismegistus, 202–3
Hermetic Philosophy, 134–35,
   140–41
   on creation, 40
   on end of discord, 159–60
   on Self, 147
   on separation from source, 145
   on Unity of God, 163
Hindu Scripture
   on creation, 140
   on separation from source, 145
Hindus, 172
human personalities, enemies of,
   54–55
humankind, union with God, 169

I
I.Q. (Intelligence Quotient), 72–74
idealism, 208–9
ideas, approaching new, 4–5
illness
   mental in origin, 186

   as result of beliefs, 19, 20
immortality, 149–50, 199
individuality, 68
individuals, 123
inertia, 91
inferiority, 53–54, 61
Infinite Mind, 84, 125
Infinite Person, 168
Infinite Presence, 168
Inner Kingdom, 156–57
inner life, developing, 121
Inner Teachings, 161
intellect, surrendering, 191–92
Intelligence, 18, 212
intuition, 121

J
Jeans, James, 217n 7
Jesus
   explicit instructions about
     prayer, 192
   on faith, 190
   as first to introduce spiritual
     mind healing, 184
   on immortality, 150
   on Kingdom of God, 154–56
   Kingdom as grain of mustard
     seed, 154–55
   on Kingdom of Heaven, 151,
     152–53
   Kingdom reached through
     childlike faith, 191
   parable of the talents, 31–32
   parables of, 124–25
   as practical idealist, 185
   teaching Kingdom of God
     within, 116
   teaching Kingdom of Heaven
     within, 116
   unique power of, 124
   who was, 122–23
Jones, E. Stanley, 55
Jones, R. M., 174–75

spiritual mind treatment *(continued)*
 approach to making money,
  262
 to attract good things, 256–57
 to claim wholeness, 272–73
 to connect with inner joy,
  260–61
 to deal with fear of death,
  290–91
 to discover inner perfection,
  232–33
 to dissolve obstacles and
  wrong conditions, 228–29
 to eliminate negative situations,
  240–41
 to ensure that the right things
  happen, 242–43
 to establish peace of mind,
  298–99
 to experience inspiration,
  236–37
 to experience unity with all
  life, 306–7
 to express inner perfection,
  248–49
 to find greater possibilities,
  302–3
 to find harmony, 304–5
 to find solutions, 250–51
 to free self from fear, 244–45
 to get free of bad influences,
  276–77
 to have a healthy body,
  268–69
 to heal what needs to be
  healed, 278–79
 how to give, 221–25
 to let go of problems, 300–1
 to live joyously, 296–97
 to practice nonresistance,
  254–55
 to pray for personal peace and
  world peace, 264–65

 to release invisible spiritual
  power, 246–4
 to remove blockages from life,
  230–31
 to remove obstacles, 288–89
 to save trouble, 238–39
 to straighten out life, 258–59
 to use Mental Power, 274–75
spiritual treatment, 212
spirituality, return to, 210–11
stagnation, 91
Strecker, E. A., 20
Studies of the Soul, 174
Subjective Mind, 12, 16
success, right to, 31
superiority complex, 61
Swedenborg, 124

T
Tagore, 160
Talmud, 203
 on copies of the Truth, 141
 on God, 136
 on separation from source, 145
Taoism, 202
Taoist texts
 on balance, 180
 on God, 134
 on healing, 184
 on Inner Kingdom, 156
 on Self, 146–47
Theory of Indeterminacy, 217n 2
thought
 consciously directing, 48
 maintaining a pattern of, 17
 Mind responds to, 12
 under one's own control, 9, 12
 for using creativity of Mind, 8
Tree of Life, 154
trinity, 172–73, 175
Truth
 copies of, 140–42
 direct connection to, 124–25

ABOUT THE AUTHOR

Ernest Holmes (1887-1960) was the founder of the Science of Mind philosophy and movement. Ernest Holmes's teachings are based on both Eastern and Western traditions, and the empirical laws of science and metaphysics. Science of Mind is a spiritual philosophy that people throughout the world have come to know as a positive, supportive approach to life. These ancient truths have kept pace with and proven their relevancy in today's global village and its expanding technology and warp-speed changes.

Author of *The Science of Mind*, the seminal book on his teachings, Holmes also founded the monthly periodical, *Science of Mind* magazine, which has been in continuous monthly publication since 1927.

Through lectures, radio, television programs, tape recordings, books and magazines, Ernest Holmes has introduced millions of people to the simple principles of successful living that he called "the Science of Mind." His other works include *Creative Mind, This Thing Called You, Thoughts Are*

Things, Words That Heal Today, La Ciencia de la Mente, Effective Prayer and *This Thing Called Life.*

This classic work of inspiration will show you the awesome power contained in your thoughts and words.

Foreword by
Reverend Dr. Michael Beckwith,
A Contributor to the book and DVD,
the Secret

Words That Heal Today

An Inspirational, Life-Changing Classic from the Ernest Holmes Library

Ernest Holmes

Code #6854 • $10.95

An Inspirational, Life-Changing Classic from the Ernest Holmes Library

THOUGHTS ARE THINGS

Ernest Holmes and Willis Kinnear

Code #7214 • $10.95

Discover the life-changing power of thinking in creative and self-affirming ways.

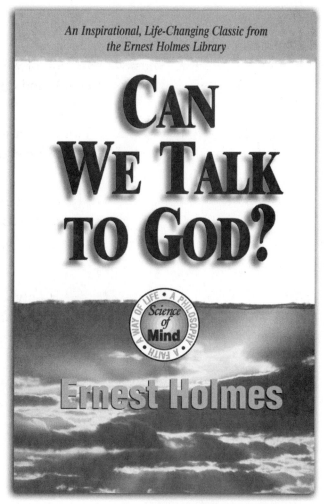

An Inspirational, Life-Changing Classic from
the Ernest Holmes Library

CAN WE TALK TO GOD?

Science
of
Mind

Ernest Holmes

Code #7362 • $10.95

Find true inner peace and a
meaningful life through effective prayer and
communion with your higher power.